AF444660

NON-EUCLIDEAN graffiti

Poems by

JOHN MUDD

I'd like to acknowledge Mikal Shively for convincing me to jump into this project. While there's not been a lot of people involved directly, I'd like to thank a few muses and heroes whom I've looked to for inspiration while I've been working on it. While my characters and references are a little of all of us, none of them is meant to be anyone on this list specifically. Okay, maybe Chuck Voss.

Kitty Bacon

M. J. Archangelini

Christine S.

Wendell Ricketts

Leslie Weifert

Chuck Voss

David Walker

Barbara Brautigam

Helen Royal

Will Sanger

Joni Dunlap

Todd Gibson

Clay and Erin Pelfrey

Gail and Doug Kaye

Jerome Frazer

CONTENTS

2024

2023

2022

Introduction

Euclid was a man, a particularly clever man that I don't know much about. Euclid is credited with conceiving the geometry of straight lines and flat planes. Generally speaking, most geometry you've studied is likely to be Euclidean.

George A. Armington was another very clever man, who lived in Euclid, Ohio. The most important thing I know about him is that he founded a company called The Euclid Crane and Hoist Co., which is primarily known for making really big earth-moving equipment. Generally speaking, any freeway you might drive on was built using dump trucks based on a design by Euclid Crane and Hoist.

My Dad was a relatively clever man, who worked in steel manufacturing some time before I was born. Above the door in our workshop was a Polaroid picture of him as a young man posing quite candidly with his pants around his ankles next to another fellow and a giant rack of Euclid axles. He was always pretty protective of that picture and tended to wipe the dust and spray-paint overspray off it from time to time. There was no shortage of notes and graffiti on those walls, phone numbers, notes, diagrams. The faded pic above the door though, was not to be defiled or removed. I never knew what kind of kinky shit my old man was into, and he sure as hell wasn't about to talk to his teenage son about it.

Years later I can understand that it's difficult to tell someone about your kinks, particularly if they seem a bit far-fetched. For me, telling my partner that I want to engage in a sexual act which involves an Elvis costume, personal lubrication, and thirty-two pounds of under ripe bananas has been difficult.

About two years ago, I started trying to write a letter spelling out the validity of my fantasies, the erotic history of Elvis Impersonators, and ideas on where to hire an appropriate videographer. As I write this, my sweetie still remains oblivious to the glorious depravity I hope we might someday engage in. I refuse to admit that after all this time I've failed to get to the point, and see it as a glorious wall documenting some most excellent side quests, even if it never gets around to the Polaroids or Euclid axles.

07-11-2024
Chico, California

2024

Bunker

04 28 24

I went to a store that sells medium to large size bunkers.
In the parking lot there was an old minivan
that had obviously been there for a while.
I found it unlocked.
There was a small spiral notebook on the dashboard.
Opening it I found
about ten different variations of a note,
written with a marker pen.
The front page edit was the most complete,
though many pages had clearly been ripped out.
"Sometimes I like to use words
like leveling up
and moving forward
as if I were my own motivational speaker.
Then there's times when I really want
to find new and innovative ways to disengage.

At one point or another I find myself unwilling
to keep up the struggle
for whatever the heck it was I hoped for.

Most of life is annoying and painful,
there's no real end to that,
but stability itself makes it tolerable.
It's easy to cope with life's crazy
when you have a warm place to sleep and plenty to eat.
The scope of our lives expands and contracts,
it's easy to give up in a moment things
that will be important to our future selves.
Sometimes we have to
give up the known for the unknown,
based on nothing more than speculation.
Sometimes we're really sure
that the repercussions of our actions will be dire,
but we just have to do them anyway."

Between the seats of the van
were a couple of Styrofoam coffee cups,
and half a pack of Marlboro cigarettes.
The rest of the van seemed to be
not so much clean as empty.
I wondered what happened
to the person that wrote such a note
and what else they might have had to say.
I thought to report the vehicle to someone,
maybe look in the glove box for any other information,
then I thought a note so profound might not be written
by someone who wanted to be found.
I looked at the tree-sap-encrusted van,
then over at the shiny black bunkers on display.

I looked to the sign above each bunker,
describing each one with its clever name,
and attributes written in big friendly letters.
Then I looked at the note.
I'm pretty sure I came
to the fancy bunker dealership looking for answers.
I had imagined these answers to take the form
of physical dimensions, specifications, pricing,
and finance options.
I left with bigger questions and a lot less interest
in shiny metal bunkers.
I looked back at the old car rusting in the parking lot,
I looked back at the names in big friendly letters.
It was time to go.

Totality Poem

04-18-24

Glen was pretty graceful for a man in his 60's
wearing thigh boots and corset.
In the low light of the hotel
he tried not to wake his lovers,
all lovely people were scattered around the room
as if arranged for some kind of movie set.
Glen had managed to locate the shiny pleather clutch
that held his rather worn wallet and keys.
He'd even located his leopard print coat,
negating the need to actually get dressed.
Hopefully there would be a stealthy drive home
after this glorious night of debauchery.
First, there was the matter of a lacy pair of black panties
that simply had to be located.
It's not as though they were worth much,
but someone gave him those panties,
someone who really liked seeing him in them.
The person that gave Glen those panties
told him they were magic.
As our reluctant hero
looked around the room at the sexy bodies,
breathing in the scent of
sweat, Final Net, and Old Spice,
it sure seemed like they were.

Glen scanned the room for movement
he felt the crevices for one particular soft satin shadow.
Anyone watching might think Glen the most glamorous,
the most bold cat burglar there ever was.
He was Silent,
his task mysterious.
He was like the letter D
in bundt cake.

Euphoria

Elio woke like most mornings,
huddled in his warm blankets
trying to determine where he was and how he got there.
Somewhere between trying to summon a memory
of the room he was in,
and piecing together the fragments of pictures
that make up his identity,
a huge man with a beard walked into the room.
The man standing over Elio carried two cups of coffee.
He sat one on the night stand
then walked out with the other.
No words were passed,
no eye contact.
Elio reasoned that this man
was familiar with his predicament
and found himself being reassured by this knowledge.
Hours later and Elio was lying awkwardly
in a slippery dentist chair,
there was some kind of tool just at the edge of his
    vision,
there was a thick plastic clamp
in a cheerful yellow hue distending his jaw.
His personal memories had returned,
so much so that he had remembered this visit to the
dentist,

as well as all the pertinent information
to get this qualified professional
to engage in this very expensive form of torture.
Staggering to a large desk
near the door to the waiting room,
the receptionist wearing pink scrubs,
proceeded to ask questions.
These were tedious questions
mostly having to do with numbers,
that could easily have been answered
by looking at the screen in front of her.
There were chopsticks holding up the bun on her head.
Elio was mesmerized at the rhythmic way they bounced
first side to side then front to back.
When the chopsticks stopped moving
he would mimic the movement they had been making,
along with a grunt.
Then the cycle started over.
Warm blankets awaited Elio and his lover,
late on a weeknight.
He loved the intimacy of their bodies
touching skin on skin.
His lover whispered something in his ear
Something truly worth remembering,
but that wasn't going to happen.

 Gap

04 14 24

Some holes are drilled precisely
and clearly to serve a purpose,
others are rough gaping openings
where purpose has been lost.
In Eighteen Fifty-One
an Architect Leopold Eidlitz
wrote a letter to a church building committee.
Like many letters to many committees
it was read aloud in a meeting,
some half-hearted decisions were made.
There was tea and very likely crumpets, nibbled upon.
The letter was mostly forgotten.
In Nineteen and Ninety-One
a young man filled out a form
as legibly as possible and a check,
to a catalogue store called Musicians Friend.
Unlike Leopold Eidlitz's letter,
it was acknowledged quickly and acted upon.
Soon a young man named Audi
would receive a Korg Prophecy.

In the Year Two Thousand and Fifteen,
a hopeful congregation bought a very old church.
This very old church had a very tall steeple.

In the year Two Thousand and Sixteen
Audi carefully explained to his local constabulary
that the sounds emanating from his trailer park home
were indeed music
and not some large furry animal in heat.
In the year Two Thousand and Twenty-Four,
the towering stone steeple of a church
designed by Architect Leopold Eidlitz
toppled with a horrendous crash
taking down beams, shingles, bricks,
and possibly an innocent pipe organ.
The letter written in Eighteen Fifty-One
outlined the inevitably of this disaster,
and the reasons for it.
Audi had seen a lot of monuments fall
in his short time on this big blue ball.
He'd seen some deities come and go.
He'd seen the brightest minds and dullest dullards
all with ambitions and hopes,
based on a future that never came,
built from ideas that slipped away like a clever quip.
He was dwelling on the fallen steeple
and the hubris of the people that worshiped beneath it.

They had a dream so grand
that they named their settlement
after one of the biggest cities they knew.
There's footage of the steeple falling
but that doesn't express the end of the story

marked with the giant hole where the music
and the message once emanated.
He tried to fathom the very moment of failure.
What would it sound like?
He was almost finished with his cigarette
when a pigeon shit on his head.

Derision

04-01-24

Algorithms are much like gods.
Maybe they're helpful in a moment,
but usually they are not.
There's a whole galactic overarching view,
unfathomable statistical calculus,
and the historical perspective given by omnipotence.
Given all this you'd think all these gods and algorithms
could just complete simple tasks like rigging an election,
or playing the song I just barely remember
written by some guy
that's about his favorite kind of cheese.

I guess in the end
they do have an agenda to push,
to make the most popular thing
even more popular with all of us.

Still it would seem
that after I've listened to sixteen dronescapes in a row,
then listened to minimal modular improvisations
for about the time it takes to wash two loads of laundry,
a god or an algorithm might surmise that
I'm not likely to be disposed to enjoy the stylings
of a preteen boy
imparting the nuance of his "real playa life."

"La la la selling weed,
La la la la I like titties"

There once was a function of search and result
where one could search a term
like "concerto for oboe and theremin"
and a screen full of results
would magically appear before you.
You could simply play them in order
as if they were songs in a list which in fact they were.
Progress happens,
people change
and so do gods and algorithms.

I can now play a selection from my search,
ideally a jaunty composition played on an oboe,
accompanied by a theremin,
then expect the next bit of music,
after a jingle about a cream for psoriasis,
to be a slow cover of some song
from Metallica, sung badly
by someone whose name is a car they can't afford.

Bathtub

03 07 24

I make some strange things from time to time.
What I'm making now is a glib observation,
spawned by existential disdain.
I can hear the gurgle of the now-cold bath water
running down the drain.
It's a teasing reminder that soon
I'll be sitting in an empty bathtub
probably shivering,
too lost in a moment that's already passed
to stand upright.
Time doesn't travel in a straight line
nor at a constant speed.
A drum beat gets annoying
without a change in tempo
or some kind of break.
Maybe we grow to need that annoyance
maybe it's just buoyancy.
Similarly this concept might apply
to the department of motor vehicles
or the dentist.
Some rhythms' schedules and itineraries
go on and on relentlessly.
Time passes quickly

running a simple circuit
from one goal to the next.
Then there's those times of wonder
when where we were
and where we might be
are less defined.
Good or bad we may remember those fills,
those gaps, variations
far past the curve
where we are no longer
the person having the experience.
I think that the rhythms,
the beats the steps
are as important as the glorious gaps between them.
Sometimes as I look at the strange phases
that become a life
I can't help but think of it as a bit of music,
a graph, a rhythm, a series of movements.
A guitar solo just doesn't ring the same
without a few verses about some existential crisis.
A cum just isn't the same without a bit of depravity.
A punchline isn't the same without a story.
Unless of course it involves a bowling ball
or a rubber boot.
Time-specific commitments,
spatial commitments,
goals make up the rhythm of our lives.

There's a towel hanging by the sink
that seems so far out of reach
of my corporeal mass
and my will to leave this tub.
Needs must, I arise
with no small amount of trepidation.
I have to write this down.

Yeam

02 23 24

He took a sip of wine slowly, deliberately.
The glass was in his hand mostly as a prop,
he was trying to remember the name
of a campsite he visited a few years ago.
It was a person's name,
maybe someone from the local lore?
Maybe it was the name of the people
they displaced to build it.

He was sitting on very expensive-looking white couch
watching a couple of drunk straight people fucking
on the glass-topped coffee table.
Every so often they would stop grunting
long enough to steady themselves
from tumbling onto the floor.

He felt himself trying to look interested
in the show before him.
He tried to fix his face
pleasant enough not to seem scornful,
but not so interested
that he might be asked to participate.
The space was cramped;
loud incoherent conversations
only drunk people have.

Too much anxiety to be genuinely bored,
he was imagining long highways, high cliffs.
His mind wandered to where it was calm,
where the scale of it all
left a lasting sense of awe.

Eventually one of these drunk people
would fall onto him and his perch
knocking the red wine onto the white couch,
he'd excuse himself,
to push past the bodies,
into the kitchen for a towel,
ritual wiping of the white vinyl
would preface a slow gracious exit.
For now though,
He could only hold this pose,
he anticipated this move,
and rehearsed it in his mind.
A socially stalwart exit
to this drunken sloppy sexual limbo.

That's it!
The campsite was in limbo!
Limbaugh Canyon Trail!
Everything was going to be okay.

Pay odie

02 22 24

It won't be long
before people think of the year twenty twenty
the way I think of nineteen twenty.
I'm planning to buy five sets of identical outfits
to wear every day to the office.
It's pointless to engage in self-expression.
Of course by making such a choice
I'm still expressing myself,
just differently.
I'm going to begin my journey
by studying pictures
of a museum-style chastity belt being made.

No one talks about events on March first
being a day late on leap years.
This is my first bondage-related woodworking project,
thus I would like some praise,
admonishment.
I would also like advice
on what to charge
for a twenty-two-second custom creampie vid.

Why do dudes over 40 all have stories
about finding porn in the woods?
If I found porn in the woods

I probably wouldn't bother telling a story about it.
Maybe I have and I just don't remember.
Looking for something wank worthy in my local library.
Someone was making noise a few aisles over.
Stern warnings.
That's not allowed.
Nothing is as quiet as sleeping,
that's not allowed either.

Odie needed to make a decision;
keep the car or turn it in for a full refund.
This was a teaching moment.
It's very fortunate that eating
is a rather enjoyable activity
considering how often we have to do it.

Someone asked me to compile
a comprehensive list of social platforms
based on their overall toxicity.
I just can't remember who or why.

There's a video called "Manifest Your Gay Dream Life."
No matter how many times I watch it,
I still have to get off the couch,
often putting on clothes
in order to get tacos.
My gay dream life seems far away.

It's not really clothing,
it's not really being dressed.
It's also not really sex

if you're the only one there.
This isn't truly naked
and it wouldn't in and of itself
put your content into the bondage niche.
Though with other elements
of sexual shenanigans
it might.

I guess in the end there's more emphasis
on porn than star.
Often people dedicate a special room
in their house to get some freak on,
they refer to it as a sex dungeon.
I imagine it adds to the overall gestalt,
but it's not as if it's going to be mistaken
for any other kind of dungeon.
Lawd!

How many dungeons do you really need?

I'm sure that if you asked Phil
about his being a porn star
he'd take some kind of issue with the title.
While he lays prostrate on the floor,
his prostate bearing the brunt,
amidst the moans and grunts
a blunt oversized silicone phallus
driving in and out of him
like a jackhammer journeyman
with a brand new Hilti.

I make music and a few other things,
and when I'm tired and feel like a wank
before bedtime I bed down beneath the blankets
and begin the porning process,
watching Phil passionately filling an orifice or two
and imagine some profoundly implausible scenario
where I might join him in the revelry.
I eventually reach some dopamine-induced euphoria.
Then awash in post-occurrence clarity
I imagine how many fellas I see on a regular basis
might be engaging in some spectacular hobby
they generally don't talk about.
Next week he'll be making another vid.
Next week I'll be writing another rant.
Maybe it'll be another about Phil.
Creation is something we just have to do.
We have to,
because we can.

Tequila Confessions

02 21 24

Let's talk a little bit about the music I'm uploading tonight, which depending on the context by which you're reading this, could seem like a return to source or a completely bonkers collection of half finished stream of consciousness. Consciousnesses?

Today a nearly eighty-year-old man was gifting me with his insights into the state of local politics. I've tried to portray a sense of what this sounded like in my head as he led up to some crescendo where he took to beating on the hood of the customer's car I was trying to tune up, while telling me that if I didn't vote for his favorite candidate it's actually tantamount to murder, and I would surely be condemned to the hellfire-like realm of the eternally condemned.

I started this piece of music with audio hacked from some vintage porn where a woman writhes around a hotel room fondling her lingerie-wrapped breasts, while maniacally telling you what a loser you are for watching so much porn. I used a stretch algorithm to slow her down to half speed, so she sounds even more drunk and demented. I took this as a baseline to run from channel five in the mixer into channels six, seven, and seventeen. Channel seventeen has my stash of absolutely chaotic plugins and presets that I've taken to calling Terry.

To try and simulate the sharp pain that comes from the stress-induced crick in my neck I decided to take the tempo which began at about ninety beats per minute, then melded the melancholy digit into an automation track in the shape of a hockey stick then clicked that into measure-length machinations, and put them into a random order, so that while the scornful remarks of Mistress Something-Or-Other are almost coherent, she randomly breaks into high-pitched squeaks. Terry was then given the task of distorting and repeating these squeaks in the most cringe-inducing way.

Riding the relentless throb of misguided misogyny I set some reverberations and echoes to de-enunciate the vowels to create a whalesong like wail out of well selected times that required a painful application of maths. Somewhere between fifty and one hundred milliseconds the blathering goes from a sense of ethereal majesty to that of simple repetition. I really don't know how this works, but I had a pretty good idea down deep in my heart. I really didn't know how this worked, but I wasn't going to let that stop me from pulling chaos from the hexahedron of obsession. I then took about two hours to watch a decidedly uninspired documentary about the history of high-heeled shoes.

As the credits rolled I found myself wondering about the validity of my life's decisions. After that existential crisis I remembered what I was trying to accomplish, and took to creating a crazy chord progression in the form of a piano roll. I set up a series of software synths to presets that were printed as pads. I made some other adjustments to my mellow waveforms but I really can't be bothered to try and remember what they were.

Speaking of things I can't remember, I clicked and dragged on hundreds of icons, and made progressively fine adjustments with the fantasy that there was some sense of direction I was trying to adjust to. I was in essence having a dream about having some profound passionate dream. Well that's what I suppose I was doing, I don't honestly remember.

I'd like to thank all the participants, people and animals alike that frolic like a nun named Maria in the cranial airspace I call my mind. You're the wormy deals that form the monster eyelids that keep me going.

How Do I Simplify the Transition?

02-14-24

Behold the ritual music of Odo Island,
Watch the trucks and camera crews
unpack and stretch out.
Be annoyed at the sound
of the person yelling into a bullhorn.
Notice the roads blocked off, the lights, the booms.
Godzilla is coming to Odo Island, real or virtual.
Akira Ifukube writes the music
that brings Godzilla to life.
Akira Ifukube made the monsters roar.
Over 250 bits of music put to film,
Snow Trail, a forgotten bit of celluloid
puts him on the path.
Godzilla flares in a scarlet chain reaction.
Osaka up in flames.
Fighter planes scurry to stop the carnage,
or maybe to add more fodder.
People die, planes crash, buildings crumble.
Godzilla still advances.

More planes, more bombs, machine guns, smoke rises,
a model tank looks menacing
in situ behind some trees.
Godzilla Legend II—Voyage to Dream Quest
plays on cassette,
on a dust-covered boom box in the corner of my shop.
I've been crouched beneath a tractor,
an oil change and a five-hundred-hour service.
How long had I been there,
watching the stream of oil,
wondering blissfully at the music of *Godzilla*?
Picture the orchestra and conductor,
overblown horns giving voice to a terrible monster
that didn't as yet exist.
Those reeds playing unison trills,
screeching in minor keys,
what must they have thought of the cacophony,
leaping from the score.
All those people are gone.
Godzilla lives on,
undefeated by time.
I sit up from my work,
I've been here long enough that my legs don't move.
A lone vocalist sings a lofty refrain.
A Japanese man stands in the center of the door,
he's a silhouette in the strange blue light of sunset.
He's been watching me.

How long has he been there?
He's about to ask me a question.
A long awkward silence passes,
while I attempt to get my legs to move.
While I try to convince myself he's really there.

No Substitutions Please

02 05 24

It's just not the same!
Like the difference between manufactured diamonds
   and mined ones.
It's the suffering that makes them special.

chapter House

02 02 24

I joined a Westclox collectors' collective.
The guy there said I was looking hectic.
I just sighed.
I sipped some wine.
What does hectic mean?

He asked if I was a Westclox owner,
I said not since I've gotten older.
He just sighed.
Did I waste his time?
I was just about to talk
about my Nana's clocks.
That's when he cut me off.

I felt like I'd reached an alternate dimension,
lost track of social convention.
Obsessive behavior,
this was now the rule.
We talked as if our words were being timed.
We spoke louder and faster, stories misaligned.
I was out of wine.
This was fine.

He went on about early alarm knobs,
then the point of the story was a missing washer.

Then I glimpsed crazy in his eyes.
He asked if I knew about bell end covers.
I said no, but I have a bellend brother.
I thought I was being clever.
He picked something off his sweater,
then said fine,
I'll just show you mine.

He said I seemed to have a thirst for knowledge,
then asked about horological college.
I said no,
maybe I might go.
That's a big step for a rank beginner.
I realized I seemed a bit over eager.
I just sighed
and got another glass of wine.

Residue

01 30 24

"Aren't you supposed to have wings or some such?"
"I'm not that kind of chicken."

I watched a video the other day
of a fellow giving a presentation and tutorial
on the finer points of a Korg Volca Nubass
while just in the other room,
a much older man dangled his cock
in front of his own camera.
There's a lesson to be learned here,
but it's far beyond my understanding.

There's a birthday cake in the break room
decorated to look like a pack of Marlboro cigarettes.
It says "Happy Sixty-Ninth Birthday Peggy."
I don't know who Peggy is.
In fact this cake makes me think
there's really a lot of things I don't know.

He was trying to come up with
some innocent sounding scenario
for what he was doing with his friend Dorene
and her dad.
He started with a few half sentences,
as if some epic story was about to come to mind.

I would have just left, they're consenting adults,
and I had been on my way to have a pee,
when I heard the racket they were making.

Now I was willing to hold off a little longer,
I wanted to hear the ridiculous story
being formed behind those awkwardly blinking eyes.
Finally the awkward silence drew on long enough
that one of them couldn't stand it any longer.
"It's Crisco,
I know it's a mess
but I know how to get it out of the carpet.
No problem."

A Plethora

01 17 24

She makes a living writing ads
and box blurbs for adult novelties.
She once spent a month writing an instructional
    pamphlet
for a butt plug shaped like a cabbage.
She and her girlfriend
were looking for a quaint country home, in Cocks,
south and west of Goonhavern.
The girls hoped to find a small barn conversion
with plenty of kitchen space, and an office.
They found a real estate agent who spoke passable
    Cantonese,
but always seemed to be struggling to form sentences.
She mostly wanted to see houses of wood and stone.
She wanted ceiling beams, she wanted bricks.
She wanted to live in an old place,
far away in every way
from the metallic starship where she grew up.
She wanted to live on a planet
where most of the sentient inhabitants
are bipedal and have only one head.

She read about Cornwall,
and always dreamed of living there,
where local stores sold clothes
that only have one head hole.
People all wore shoes,
because none of them knew how to levitate.
She had high hopes of living where,
even if the people weren't like her,
at least it wasn't so obvious.

2023

Haunted Constellations

08 13 23

A lot of firsts today.
A lot of personal growth.
A lot of things to think about.
This poem doesn't rhyme.

First time an audience left alive.
My first honest review,
first time I thought that I could do better.
Today was the very first time.

First time using FL Studio Mobile.
First time I've made music at work.
The crotch ripped out of my trousers today,
this wasn't the first time.

Buchla, Fran, and Ollie

08 10 23

My ten and 14 year old cousins
asked me if I follow Python Scripting.
How do I say no
without disappointing?
This isn't really related to this song
but I started using SextPanther
and thought you lot
might find it as funny as I did.
My wife got a new haircut,
now she looks like my Mom.

I've loaded an empty project
and loaded the sound
of a washing machine
full of squeaky toys
being pushed
down a steep embankment.
I had imagined there would be more magic.

Is There Ambiance in Ambien

08 01 23

For me it's bloom and ambient occlusion.
I love my husband
but his friend writes the fun prescriptions.
I can't turn the washing machine off.
This will be my first experience
so he's got to be really really hung.

A study found that recommendation algorithms
don't work so well for hip hop artists
but for ambient artists it does.
While I'm mostly okay with his not being a furry,
I just wish he would at least wear the rabbit ears.

Right now my phone is moving in my hand,
it's like the corn syrup is moving through the screen.

You are listening to a police scanner,
that or a washing machine,
I don't remember,
it sounds very blue.

I have SoundCloud on dark mode.
It looks like your song is swimming
through the darkest depths
of a truly untidy swimming pool.

You can unplug the wire from the wall,
but probably not the hoses.
It's hard to say the word sublingual
with a mouth full of Flintstones Chewables.
The three seconds of a song
that's played after a foul ball
is really, really brutal.
If they didn't want Monopoly in the freezer
they wouldn't make it look like a pizza.
The *X-Files* music had me wondering
what's going on with Scientology?
Mexico has its own ambient music.

Captain Jack Darkness

08 01 23

My friend from Ottawa,
he takes pictures of melted butter.
He says that shoe salesmen don't get paid enough.
He gave me a cookie jar that looked like Burt Reynolds,
but he doesn't really know who Burt Reynolds is.
One day last week we went to the movies,
at least I think we did, we were really high.
There was a sexy substitute teacher
that replaced an english teacher that was killed by
   a UFO.
This sexy space chick did research on a nerdy student,
it involved lasers and an anal probe.
Soon all the cheerleaders wanted to know him,
for reasons of the plot I guess. I don't know.
It was an alien sci-fi coming-of-age adventure,
like a spandex-clad vampire Buffy show.

Since then I haven't seen my friend from Ottawa.
Maybe he's an alien and I just made him up.

Many Miles to Modular

08 01 23

Trying to get back to my roots a bit.
I'm trying to hone a craft.
I'm trying to find familiar waters.
I'm trying to get to the heart of it.
I'm thinking that maybe
that's too much to ask.

How do I find
the file I tried to download?
In what folder might it be?
It's some kind of crime.
How did I lose the thing that highlights
just what's out of key?

I'm drawing conclusions,
I'm drawing a blank.
I'm drawing a crowd,
when I visit the bank.
I'm pursuing a delusion,
that the ship hasn't sunk.

I want to make a model
of the monster from my nightmares
from wire and sticky tape.
I want to emulate my heroes,
I want to be my own man.
I want to take life easy,
just as fast as I can.

WWHD what would Hainbach Do

How do I link sounds to specific keys?
I just spent an hour scrubbing spray paint off my van.
Do you have personal issues with snow blowers?
Is dating even real anymore?
There's still time to get tickets for our Cranial Prolapse
    show.
Time waits for no man unless that man is Hainbach.

She said we have trouble communicating
we are both shallow and two-dimensional.
I said something about how radar
encompasses three physical dimensions
as well as that of time,
but the result is displayed
on a small flat circular screen.
She said I was missing her point,
I asked where her point might be on a given y axis.
She said I was wearing two different colored socks.
I said so is Hainbach.

Why does saying "Rancho Cucamonga"
make me laugh?

I'm fortunate enough to have had a Big Mac
while gazing at really big mountains.
Isn't it strange that people use disbelief
to describe repulsion?
Does it really need to be so huge?
Is population age data
inverse to population suicide data?
The largest consumers of tobacco
do not live near the largest producers of it,
and that is a shame.
The knowledge of these things is held by
   Hainbach.

Drums For Sale

07 27 23

Behold! one of the leading entertainment agencies
with over 30 years
experience servicing discerning
corporate and private clients worldwide.
He had no idea why he was there
unless someone had seen him come out
of the gay sauna.
You drop beats on it,
maybe a few synth patterns,
then move to the next.

Our business is now seeing an upturn
so we are taking this opportunity
to review our current database
of musicians and entertainers.
I was hesitant to purchase this
but now I want one in every color.
I look forward to considering your
submission.

If you have a passion for performing
and want to showcase your skills
in an unforgettable setting,
this opportunity is for you!
I took a chance assuming

that the material in this suit
should be adequately stretchable.
The search continues
as the Bottoms Up Club
auditions more of the world's best drummers.

Drommer Auditions

07 20 23

I felt like the nutty professor
with how many orgasms I had.
While the main chemical these pumps
are designed for is Diesel Exhaust Fluid,
which is a urea-based chemical
and is typically mixed 32.5 percent urea
and 67.5 percent deionized water.
Although I still douche, I usually only have to do one
　　cycle and I'm good.
We use a direct current from a battery
and it works great.
This was the first sex toy I've bought,
and it's definitely not a beginner.
My only gripe is I wish that it was waterproof
so we could leave it outside
but the connections do not look watertight.
You need a means to unload it from the semi
but we just used a rollback truck.
However, when you're not part of the gay community
and you search for men's fiber
without reading the fine print,
you're going to hear jokes from anyone
rummaging through your medicine cabinet.

A Cool Night on the Moped

07 13 23

Tammy was a bigger nerd than me,
she had freckles.
The mighty Puch Maxi
made us smell like a lawn mower.
Taco Bell is the only place
where you can find
a brand new Mercedes,
a vintage Mercury Topaz,
and two teens on a moped,
in the same queue.

499 to 23 BPM

07 06 23

Here's another cyberspace stage,
this time showcasing
how busted zero Jump deceleration is.
Does Bremsstrahlung happen
when scattering takes place?

Throw a catalytic converter in a pond and you'll get
    ripples,
is the catalytic converter made of ripples?
Maybe given enough time
all stolen exhaust components
turn to ripples.
Maybe we're all fools
and none of it matters.

I narrowly dodged death
when some idiot merged into me.
Since they are so advanced,
they'll likely be leaking radio signals
many orders of magnitude
stronger than ours.
Modern ICE vehicles still emit nitrogen dioxide
which is always an issue.

Third gear clunking,
should I still do a track day?
Military vessels are equipped with
Alcubierre drives while civilian traffic
use static wormhole stations
to traverse established shipping lanes.

I don't think she knows
the meaning of prolonged deceleration.
Maybe it's possible for matter, or energy
to travel faster than its local light due to moving
    through some highly refractive or dense material.

Sirius, the brightest star
is over eight light years from Earth.
The real fun comes
when you experience time dilation
at velocities close to C.

Why Don't You Just Jack off

06 29 23

Ready to get degraded tonight?
I would love a lube the consistency of mayonnaise.
Drumsticks are ice cream cones,
named after a cut of poultry,
which are in turn named after a musical instrument.

If your dick doesn't impress us
we'll take turns kicking you in the balls.
I don't know if you've ever tried weed lube,
It's coconut oil based.
Entering your email to unsubscribe
seems like a trap.

My husband went to a basketball game.
Is it safe to ingest a small bit of X-lube?
Isn't a light switch also a dark switch?

Tell me how useless you feel
after being unable to fuck me.
I've made up a few batches of Male Cobeco,
it always ends up feeling stringy.
Mommy is bored and wants to
control a good cuck with her small penis.

I just launched a line of vegan,
water-based lubes to make the bedroom more fun.

You won't see my pussy until you eat your own cum.
Should a bottom guy be wearing womens' panties
if he's not really a femboy?

Tonight you will face degradation, trepidation
consternation, perturbation, and delineation.
Getting slapped on the ass is either romantic,
platonic, mischievous, or corporal.

It's absurd that water isn't a solution to dry skin.
Time to get your face under my ass mid-workout.
You may already own the underwear you'll die in.

Galactic Detour

06 22 23

This sounds to me,
like the least divergent thing I've done in a while.

I got the hookup on that real inhalant.
That shit your anesthesiologist gives you.
We take your marketing and sales data
paired with powerful software,
to make absolutely meaningless statements.
My husband and I are part of a closed poly triad.
We have the same girlfriend.
How do I handle a homeless encampment
getting started up against my back fence?

I'm a pansexual cis fem sissy,
my identity sounds like a kind of coffee.
Ten inches hits differently when it stays in.
I made a few dresses this week.

I'm offering a free massage
to any cis het female who can play freebird
on the harmonica while my boyfriend dances.
I'm getting "too good to be true" vibes,
what will everyone think?

This is something I see come up occasionally
I imagine it's relatively common.

I offer pre-booked specials, outdoor adventures,
and social dates to encourage this time together.

When building a secure attachment
how do you recommend deconstructing
the relationship escalator as a stand in
for secure attachment?

I'm looking for guys who would like
to share some magic moments
with a young bottom twink named Larry.
I'm British so I love tea.

Twinkle Twinkle

06 15 23

He wanted to create music
that was both mathematically interesting and pleasing,
so he used Euclidean geometry,
and a shitty piano.

To create a more complex rhythm,
the pulses can be arranged in a non-uniform pattern,
with some pulses closer together than others.

Stroke, speed, evaluation rate, interval time,
and alternation time can be adjusted arbitrarily.
The perfect sex machine.

In this context, the Euclidean pattern
will dictate the syncopation of notes,
not their pitches.

As you didn't explain how you're doing this,
in hardware or software,
it's hard to get specific.

Is it really about discipline and being punished?
It's one of those kinks that are multifaceted,
and people have very specific relationships with it.

This gasket is meticulously manufactured
to ensure proper fit and seal performance,
reducing the need for maintenance and repairs.

As the hood pins wear
closing the hood may become more difficult
lining up the latches can become frustrating.

Like many ancient Greek mathematicians,
Euclid's life is mostly unknown.
He is accepted as the author of four mostly extant
    treatises.

Archimedes and Apollonius vaguely reference his
    existence.
Archimedes strangely uses an older theory of
    proportions,
rather than that of Brian Eno.

Confessions of an Instigator

06 09 23

Larry reached under the floorboards,
and handed the familiar jar to Tom.
Tom then put some of the
colorless lubricant on my dick.

Simar, you're breaking the car,
Simar!?

The first overture happened a day or two later.
One thing led to another and the next thing I knew
I was wandering around Castro Street
dragging a mannequin behind me.

I'll bet that burns later.
Don't put your dick where the fuel goes.
Tom looked at me the way an old dog
looks at a dropped english muffin.

Simar asked Larry, the new boy,
to tell us about himself.
His family had always wanted a girl.
There was this one time though.

Attending a Party with a Toothache

06 01 23

I attended a party with two hundred people last night,
and I need to tell others about it.
I'm recruiting guys for an upcoming gangbang scene,
there will be fancy coffee.

I still dream of attending a kink party,
being handcuffed all night.
I've been the drunkest guy at two of his events.
He'd better be the drunkest at mine.

What do you think of hairstyles,
for attending an orgy?
Are you a reseller in the Las Vegas Area?

After they tied the knot,
my favorite sims moved into a new house.
Does cunnilingus hurt if you have a toothache,
a moderate one with dull throbbing pain?
Like what does it do to your jaw?
Will I need a safeword?

Cher attended Carol Burnett's birthday,
all by herself, except for her entourage of course.

We moved to a new area since I left the church.
I want to make a good impression
at the company christmas party,
I've only worked there a week.

"Bet you miss every inch of this huh!?"
he texted with a dick pic that clearly wasn't his.
I'm going to a farewell party,
I want to look more stylish.
I want to look like I just arrived
from a better party.

Take a Chance Slowly

05 25 23

Take a chance on me,
Take it slowly like really really slowly.
It sounds really epic when you say it that way.

I'm firmly on team swan gown,
she laid an egg and the egg was her purse.
It's an homage to Marlene Dietrich.

A cross-dressing pilgrimage,
Tonight we're in Alice Springs,
where the queens of the desert once sat.

It's not a feel good movie,
It's set in the nineties.
*The Incredibly True Adventures
of Two Girls In Love.*

Two thousand eleven gave us *The Book of Mormon,
Love Never Dies, Catch Me If You Can,
Sister Act,* and *Priscilla, Queen of the Desert.*

It's harrowing and heartbreaking.
It's one of my favorites for the way,
it depicts the aftermath.

The agent told the cop
"No lieutenant,
your men are already dead."

They Made the Zombies

05 18 23

They made the Zombies in *Resident Evil 2* really thick.
Your little pony is a bit shy so be gentle at first.
What do you have in your tip menu?
Eyebrow hair is
the only universally agreed on facial hair.
I enjoy my sleeve but she doesn't really look
like the Venus of Willendorf.
Can you make it so just one fan
has to pay to message you?
I'm 35 and playing with my favorite toy again.
When I register for an account it asks me for my address.
My husband told my sister
about the wedding of our daughter
and I refused to let their family stay at our house.
The 5 amp/hour battery cuts out after five minutes of use.
I have an important release tonight
but I can't find my keys.
I hate this app but I'm stuck with it.
I typically run my mower without turning on the
    self propel.
They are looking for construction site coordinators.
This is a bit ranty but
I am so sick of hearing that dinging noise
every time I go to open the tailgate.

NyQuil and Cough Drops Part A

04 29 23

I want to tell my parents about NyQuil dreams.
The girls dropped the pod at 3am,
when I recovered it, the guest was D. B. Cooper.
Only in a few dreams did I wear a dress.
My dream world has buses and trails,
to make travel between nightmares more efficient.

I'm limited with the appropriateness of movies.
You're not a loser,
leaving a live-in relationship is really hard.
What do allergists do when they can't function?
We were in the back of the house,
there were tiny doll hands littering the floor.

Maybe you should talk with your therapist
before bringing it up with your parents.
DayQuil and NyQuil will join the battle,
replacing the Randomize button.
I'm going to try and participate in some low-stress
social activities where I feel safe.
In real life I've been thinking about getting a new
   dentist.

Why does this mirror have prominent butt cheeks?
Why are you obeying the sun,
when it commands you to lose consciousness?
The more exhausted the more vivid the NyQuil
    dream.
I just thought it important for context.

Those two empty spaces make me want to sob.

NyQuil and Cough Drops Part B

05 04 23

Common sense is rarely common
and never really makes sense.
I love this shirt.
I would be on my knees with legs spread
so vertical adjustment just isn't as important.

There may be more people in the world
wearing wool than sheep.
Cheers to not covering your arms,
legs, or tummy this summer.
I want it to hold a fleshlight,
or similar case with sleeve.

Falling asleep is weird,
you simply lie there until you lose consciousness.
I call them my "Can't Touch This" pants.
Thrusting creates more force than anal.

Service industry jobs must have gotten away
with some sketchy stuff before the internet.
I have a weakness for cowl-neck dresses,
but I don't think I pull them off very well.
All hail the inventor of duct tape.

Sociology is the only academic discipline
written by the object of the study,
with an ideally subjective bias.
Rompers are becoming my new favorite.
I became addicted to it in a very short time
and now rub it on my cock every time it rains.

Imagine the CPU that this reality runs on.
I felt cute and summery with all these flowers.
This machine has made me so much sluttier
and I love it.

When you cut a corner
you create two new corners.
I have a meeting with a talent agency on Sunday,
I was thinking of wearing a fez.
I'm straight and have never experienced a real dick.

As your waiter leaves with your order
you become the waiter.
This is a pretty light outfit,
but I know I'll be overly warm later.
I've never been spelunking,
should I go for the free chimney descent?

Raquel Welch

04 28 23

Do most people use the e-Pedal?
Is it that dangerous to drink lake water?
The *Fantastic Voyage* actress and sex symbol
was eighty-two.
Maybe mules aren't sexy and ruin an outfit.
I asked the server for advice,
he pulled up a chair and explained the dishes to me.

Somewhere someone's Tinder date didn't show up
because they died, and the person never knew.
My first celebrity crush is gone.
He spent years tunneling through a wall in his cell,
covering the hole with a poster of Raquel Welch.
The comment makes it even better.
I just received a shipment of handmade cotton hoodies.

Clean fibers will always move more freely.
Coming up next I'll interview Raquel Welch
about Johnny Carson.
That list includes a lot of people.
I put an asterisk in because many
were forced to pass as white to get work.
She told me about Jerry's mechanic.
She's a spy but also a skydiver, so there's action.

Morning in a Strange Body

04 20 23

As he'd been instructed, Sam told the man at reception that he was here to visit his uncle. For most people hypnopompic hallucinations are considered normal and are not cause for alarm. Trees talked to me about humans on magic mushrooms. They have personalities and gender too.

I filled in a survey at the library.

It was the most bizarre experience of my life.

Generally hallucinations are sensory experiences that don't correspond to what's happening.

I started feeling so calm and loved and I began seeing a bit more clearly.

Experiencing hypnopompic hallucinations for the first time you might wonder if they are a cause for alarm.

Once I'm in your gorgeous body we can make our way to your family farm for a long weekend getaway.

She unbuttoned her tiny shorts, and breathed a deep sigh.

Three or four objects fell out.

The nature of hypnopompic hallucinations differs from the nature of mental illness.

It is simultaneously ironic and sad that so many teachers
are terrible with children. Sacrificing yourself for
your clone is both a selfish and selfless act.

It's possible that I'm a hypochondriac
and I don't even know.

Ants Have Crawled Across Your Genitals While You Slept

04 14 23

Ants have crawled across your genitals while you
   slept.
I'm losing my mind over simple math.
Maybe God should be an elected position.
It's hard to press clay truly flat.

Do you have a perfect dress?
No woman wears trail runners outside of the trail.
Someone suggested white sneakers.
I have a pair of red converse as my holy grail.

That's the *SS Catala,* it was wrecked in Washington.
The things I've found at my job are amazing.
Where are the truly exhaustless air conditioners?
I get really horny swimming in a muddy lake.

Some dainty gold jewelry would look quite nice.
I'm on the "no new shoes" train this week.
I've never done this kind of thing before.
I've nothing to wear while I clean.

Joyous Life

04 06 23

I'm at the lowest points of my life.
Anyone want to play with an octagonal femboy?
I was out with my friends
playing a game
late at night
and we all just randomly
started feeling anxious
and weirded out.

There's always so much concern
about Halloween candy,
there's nothing about Easter eggs.
Why is Jesus portrayed as caucasian
when he's from the middle east?

There should be a name for men
who donate sperm to sperm banks.
Have a homosexual man and woman
ever become lifelong romantic partners?
Current mileage at the halfway point
of our thirty-eight-hundred-mile trip,
thirty-nine point one.

Karaoke songs have the most random images.
Mexico might have been better off
if the United States had won the war.
Which one do you want to be?
Spit accumulates in my mouth when I sing.

What are Kool-Aid Bursts?
You've only got twenty minutes
to make something tasty.
You can never step on your shadow.
Humans evolved to prefer patterns
even when there aren't any.

While My Banjo Gently Weeps

03 24 23

The Quirkiest person I ever knew came from Uruguay.
Bella has started playing *The Last Of Us*.
Since when do we not count the source as canon?
Only the first one had a story in mind.
The quality is there in One.
She has flashbacks in *The Fruit of Grisaia*
and she shows up again in *The Billion Dollar Hobo*.

I told my cousin he got me pregnant
as an April Fools joke,
he was so scared ha ha ha ha ha ha!!!
How did you notice he wasn't turning the wheel?
Driving backwards is half the job anyway.

How do I simulate Mic input from files?
Should I be worried about getting pregnant?
I could possibly be having a mental problem?
What health precautions should I take,
if I work somewhere that regularly deals with firearms?

No matter how much he cries,
never feed him after midnight.

The good news is that if all the banks collapse
you'll only be out about three fifty.
There is currently a shortage of people in the trades
because older workers are retiring and there is a lack
of young people entering the trades.

There is a Japanese term for exercising under the sun.
They want to rehabilitate an area of society
where crime is ingrained in the culture.
Technically every house is a homeless shelter.

Rhythmic Dysphoria

03 22 23

This is the sound of two drum machines,
battling for dominance,
falling further and further out of sync,
eventually being fired out of a cannon,
into a factory that makes cuckoo clocks.

I was conceiving a story,
of a wealthy oil tycoon from Texas,
who begins a passionate affair,
with three quadriplegic ladies,
who don't speak english.

Being mistaken for a male prostitute,
our hero questions his own identity.
Our hero keeps a secret.
Our hero overshares.
Our hero goes to meetings.

His rhythm is put off kilter,
his schedule is disrupted.
Slight variations
have huge consequences.
It seems a profound plot.

It's not very sexy.

LFo Doηe BrS

03 10 23

When they eat Mexican food in South America,
do they still call it Mexican food?
Why do Chinese people on TikTok talk in monotone?
Is this a sign of mental illness?
So, when do we throw bricks?
Why do parents whine?
Do tech startups have a tech starter?
Why is it that I always seem to pull tops,
like there aren't more bottoms?
If I wrote this with ChatGPT would it still suck?
Do you believe your pet should be able to talk to you?
If I dye my hair blue is everyone going to judge me?
How do I support my trans sisters?

Is it bad for me to have a burning hatred of cheetahs?
Can anyone tell me if this is how she sets up meets?
What do you think 2023 will bring?
What is the painting of the man removing a mask
to show he's sad and lonely?
Why do I feel so different when I dress up as a girl?

If I put an elephant in the room,
could I shower with my contacts in?
Were you a "gifted child"?
Would a transgender girl like flowers?

Do those people who have a lot of sex,
have more sex than the people who have less?
Why do small places like beach towns
have year round Christmas stores?

What motivates streakers?
Why do nightclubs have dress codes?
Have you ever killed a bug?
Why are we constantly asked
to leave our comfort zone?
Isn't the goal to be comfortable?
How do I change this?
Did others have this reaction to breast growth?
Is Trix really just for kids?
What age do I have to be,
to be considered smart?
What are the benefits of eating cat food?

How do I separate weeds,
from a pile of soil?
Would a transgender girl like flowers?
What does this quote mean?
Any straight guys feel like it's nice
to be submissive sometimes?
What's the weirdest place
you've given a blowjob?

Cranial Field Recordings

03 08 23

People doing role plays and calling it ASMR.
The game is controlled by thought.
I'd encourage every adult in this story
to obtain a cactus enema.
The player's CPU is connected
to a central computer
connected through a cable
plugged in at the nape of the neck.
Congratulations Cactus Girl!
You're now in the same photo
as that guy sticking his dick
into an apple pie.

It was an accident,
on the set of a Russian film.
I'll take the wicker dildo cactus.
It has more tomatoes.
Following the completion of the
Winds of Change album,
Dunbar was replaced.

Eleanor has seen her fair share of dicks
but no amount of rosaries prepared her
for administrative work.
In the department of silly walks
the charting is so onerous,
so pervasive,
that the hospital has to hire
Donny Baldwin to help me keep up.

I would have lost my mind
if when she asked the guard his name
he answered;
"Why don't you come back
when you come up with something
a little more creative
you sack of poorly packaged poo!"
It's called cranial resonance.
My mind went on
to more integrated cranial translators.

He explained the science
behind the biosignal processing discs.
That sounds horrifying
and it is.
Just to let you know ahead of time,
I'm not from the CIA.
They are nothing but twat waffles
with syrup between the cranial cavities.
I should cover up this cat stick
I got it ten years ago.

I'm personally bothered
by the room she's recording in.
All of the shelves
are just as bare and unused
as that soft tissue in her cranial cavity.
It's a clown world now
and every one gets fucked
with a cactus dildo,
and there's no lube on site.
This recording was taken
from an abandoned Warforged Lab
outpost near the south border.

Yes, the Red Scimitars
are a mixed gene-seed chapter.
There's no way this guy was ever serious.
If you're not basically fingering your asshole
when you wipe
you need help.
Initially nothing changes
as these are small animals
with little means to record information
or use tools.

Large Furry Furries

03 03 23

In a world of constipation and diarrhea,
it's perfectly okay to be an unremarkable piece of shit.
Sell smarter not harder, it's painless.
It's national mutt week.

I'm excited for the presentation
on contracts for a culinary academy.
Has anyone tried the zero turn
with the steering wheel?
This is the funniest Nick Cage thing
I've ever seen.

I still think about the friends
I'm no longer friends with.
I feel like I'd really enjoy crochet
and hope it is simpler than knitting.
I got my sweet granny to do that
with a Pixies T-shirt long ago.
We had goofy mad-libs level
artificial intelligence for years,
then suddenly it's writing coherent
and sometimes useful advice.

The dash hasn't disintegrated,
it looks a lot better, but it's still a Dodge.
After the amount he made me squirt,
I don't think I can tell my cuck
"yours is perfect and the big ones just hurt" anymore.

When I think of a platform I think of breakdowns
and how easy or difficult it would be to get parts,
get it fixed and keep moving forward.
That is not a real modeling agency.
Please try again after you've acquired more karma.

I pulled up on the freeway,
unsure of how the accident happened.
I'm looking for a place to fill water bottles.
I know there are many layers to homelessness
and maybe what I'm describing already exists
or has already been unsuccessfully explored.

Very skilled artistry,
note the butthole colors.
I am severely tempted to pay.
In a boxing ring its lungs will collapse
and it'll be crushed under its own weight.

It's just that its neck is so long,
I'm thinking I could get to it
and sustain the damage it would inflict.
The placement of the hands and the arms
connecting to the legs gives off big vulva vibes.
People call the police for stupid things all the time.

My best friend told me about this yesterday
and I thought he was trolling.
Tinky lost his winky.
She can taste what you had for dinner.
There's nothing here a paper bag won't solve,
those slappy bags hang almost as low as my standards.
Now there is a whole train of men masturbating
together at this one image.
It's all your fault.

Valentine Party

02 25 23

Build in extra time to put them on because the canvas collapses the minute a foot gets near it. We talked about that guy with the long hair and I confessed to her that I felt so confused because my body reacted in one way with him, while my mind was panicking at the idea of imagining something more romantic with him. Hopefully they will stretch out a little after a breaking in period. I used the red head to clean the roof. Attaching the rods does not require any wrenches.

Halfway home, there was this nice field that looked bathed in the golden light of the sunset and I asked him if we could stop there. I'm a hairdresser that rarely sits during a 12-hr day. The only problem I have encountered is after about 20 hours of use, one of the o-rings started to fail and the wand started to leak. I sighed and he asked me if everything was ok. Still looking at the horizon, I asked him: "What if all this is just a wild dream?"

His gentle smile was so inviting and at the same time, so incredibly full of peace that I guess my body decided to override my mind. I was pleasantly surprised at the nice quality and comfort—Will be getting another color—I'm very happy with this. I decided to try an extension wand and found him. I was only looking for extension pieces. I felt a rush of emotions going through my whole body, making me feel things I've never imagined before, as if every cell would be capable of releasing unbelievable amounts of energy. Great for little trips, but not for ones that require a lot of walking.

Dreams

The way to find the harness that will
work best for you and your needs is
to simply start trying them out.
The absorptive qualities of soluble fiber
work well to counteract the hangover effect of alcohol.
I realized that I may
have something to do with them not
being as effective as before.
You need something with a flared base
to affix it to your harness,
suction cup based dildos work great for this too.
I bought these as a gift and
they're high quality and super useful
came in a pack of two so I got one for myself.
I work for AutoZone.
This was the most common size
and to have this in arms' reach is very nice.
If you're putting it inside someone,
y'all need LUBE.
It literally gave me the confidence to bottom.

Add dietary fiber to help support healthy digestion,
while making prep time quick and easy.
Your anus exists and functions regardless

of any concept of sex, gender, and sexual orientation.
When your time on the toilet is easy, smooth, and clean,
it's quick and effortless to get ready for playtime—
And you won't feel bloated.

They make great gifts for your mechanic friends.
The teeth are fine but positive
and the product itself was heavier than I expected,
which I like.
Because bodies and preferences vary greatly,
the best choice for you is always going to be a personal
    one.
I think the product is great for the purpose
of "being ready" and appreciate it as a gay man.
Alex was amazing,
he messaged me to ask how the product was
and when I told him the carrier
had lost/stolen the product,
he apologized
and our new set got shipped to us faster than was
    originally estimated.

Your Nice Soft Hands

01 28 23

When conjoined twins dream,
are they still conjoined?
How do we look into the Universe
and attempt to find some sign of life
that we can't fathom?
How does a person know the gaps
in their own knowledge?
Does cooking with alcohol
make a difference in the flavor?
Can collecting silica gel packages
cause me any harm?
I haven't seen this before.

Would you still be charged
 in this situation?
What does it mean when your cat
stares at you until you look at them,
and then they look away?
Do you have agreements
on the kinds of dynamics
you and your partner can be in
outside the primary dynamic?
What is the average of all averages?
Fifty?

What does it mean for life to be a dream?
Do you guys have any drills you can do
to help develop softer hands?

Is it true that when you flip a dog over,
they get stuck?
Can you sense it for me?
Why does it seem like all of Reddit
is concerned over a balloon?
Are people more lonely now
or are we just more aware of it?
How many pills do you think I can take?
What jobs are unobtainable
for a person with a misdemeanor?

This isn't a fun screen to see
when you're shopping and decide
that you don't want tacos after all.
Is atheism a lack of belief in a God or Gods,
and assertion that there is no God or Gods,
or both?

Could Cupid survive a time loop paradox?
Can someone call the cops
if a woman wraps her legs around a man
to force him to finish inside?
Do you view Kink and Poly as the same,
or are they different?
How?

Which Le Creuset pieces would be essential
if I only cook vegetarian meals?
Only essentials?
Is it possible to send some photos of the item
that shows the defects?
Is hierarchy more "acceptable" in kink relationships?
What does that look like to you?
What is the best pen for a long exam?
For those of you who have love bombed someone,
did you really love that person?

Should you tip when the delivery is five bucks?

Frequency Whack-A-Mole

01 26 23

I saw an ad for a guy whose headline was
"Talented Cocksucker Here" and I was curious.
The authors used it as a metaphor to characterize
the 'flavor of the month' organization that moves quickly
from one strategic initiative to another.
Finding one might seem daunting,
but once you know where to look,
it really isn't.
Because it became popular at the carnivals and fairs,
amusement parks also wanted to get in on the game.

It's dark,
and judging by this whole set up,
something tells me I'm not the first dick he's sucked
    tonight.
In a congregation without strategic clarity the latest
    and greatest idea always captures the energy of
    leadership.
The focus of leadership shifts rapidly from one
    emerging tentacle to the next,
until all congregational leaders are quite exhausted.
A public glory hole often doesn't come with the same
    level of safety
as those in staffed sex clubs, saunas, or porn cinemas.

The object of the game
is to whack the mole on the head before it drops back
    into its hole,
and to make contact with as many moles
as possible in a two minute playing period.
One of the biggest rookie errors you can make
is not bringing a sex kit.
The typical customized branded wrap
includes a custom backlit panel,
cabinet side art,
and custom branded moles and sound.

"May I ask,
please everyone,
never insert schlongs into holes they don't belong in!"
The Captain rolled his eyes.
If you're feeling tense, your smile is going to look a
    little forced,
and you could create extra wrinkles around your
    eyes and brows.
Before visiting, groom yourself as if you were going
    on a date;
otherwise you'll find yourself rejected
by what could have been an epic casual sex partner.
In the past five years,
we have done more unique, one-of-a-kind,
branded and personalized rented Games
than all the other companies combined.

Why would you want to cause death to your sperm,
especially on a large scale?
Being groped by strange hands through the wall is
    common
and uninvited cocks appearing in front of you is to
    be expected.
It's an act removed from sexual orientation
if you really think about it.
Sort of mechanical, like a sex vending machine.

optimistic Possibilities

01 10 23

Honestly, for a second my anger at him for taking my stepfather's job was replaced with anger that he was wasting that huge cock with masturbation. Modern Brian is much sadder, more jaded, trying to inject some fun at times. When you get down to it, the lyrics are spoken from the point of view of a lonely man who's lived a long life knowing he made plenty of mistakes he can never take back. I am a little uneasy about how fast it broke, but it is my first serger. I have lessons to learn: The first being don't run with your foot up! The synth in this song is a delicious meal, Jasmin sings like a raw exposed nerve. Findom is about so much more than what's on the label. It's a non issue for me but maybe that's because I generalize and invalidate my actual experience.

I couldn't bring myself to get rid of the cattle prod, I'm still using it occasionally for small jobs but I love my upgrade. There were probably ways I could have avoided fucking him, but he was too stupid (and stupid hot) to hold him responsible for his father's choices. I want a collaboration album with you both. Damn I come back to this so often. This appears to be a rebranded and face-lifted fourteen dash seventy-eight and it took a bit of work to find it but the manual does exist!

I have no idea what half of that equipment is, but it looks really cool! I was instructed to pull out a pair of sexy panties and put them on, also to have a carrot on hand. It captures what each of you are excellent at. What blood was in his cock wasn't in his brain, and he alternatively wanted me, and maybe two legit guys that have the fetish where they want to pay. "You're so big," I said, to get him going. I recalled I was here for a reason. It didn't even come close to reliably working on lightweight stretchy fabrics. "I wish I knew you were on this before I fucked him," I said. The thread started to break and quite honestly I didn't want to spend hours trying to figure it out.

2022

Wonder and Discord

12 16 22

"I feel like this piece is a bit more than the usual tedium," he said, then proceeded to pee on the suspect's basketball shoes. This lightweight machine can be oriented however you need it. The big knob is the offset, if you're using the sensor. This wine is so filled with sweet spots that all my teeth are now black and rotten now (true story). At roughly twenty-six pounds, it's easy to take on a plane and is easy to set up wherever you need an intense fuck session.

The combination of sound textures is seemingly endless. Make sure to get a good pair of boots that fit well, and remember to adjust them as necessary so that they're comfortable and stay in place. Turn it easy to the left. When you hear the pitch changing, it's time for more lube.

Sex Toys Akimbo

12 07 22

How To Write A Good Song Description

1 - Describe Your Genre in a Few Sentences:

This bit of music was conceived as a soundtrack to some hitherto non-emergent pornography, which would meld the styles of Kenneth Anger, and Federico Fellini. Ideally these would be released in conventional high definition, as well as Bong-O-Rama. While I do have a notion of how people might listen to these soundtracks or even what kind of demographic they (you) might belong to, I also realize music has a life far beyond its origin.

2 - Cite Examples of Instruments Used in Your Music:

Almost all internal parameters can be targets for modulation. The Low Frequency Oscillator, Envelope Generator, and ASSIGN knobs are very complicated things that have a wide range of parameters to discombobulate every aspect of whatever the heck I thought I was doing at the time. The Polyrhythm Cringe Generator (PCC) utilizes sidechain compression function that ducks the volume of the bass and the line-in audio. I also used a field recording of a local garbage truck driver puking into a public urinal (thanks Yani!).

3 - Be Creative and Original:

Hmmmmmmm.

4 - Mention Artists or Events That Inspired You:

Here's some of the awesome SoundCloud artists I
listen to, that generally razz my berries.

> @muterial
> @sophiesweets
> @no-mates-ensemble
> @overstate
> @blink-twice-archival
> @boson_spin
> @minimal_drone_grl
> @xxxavier-dj
> @6xek7jmktjwm

5 - Find Good Keywords for Your Songs:

- Audio output
- Adjustable parameters
- Tap tempo
- Slots
- Open source design
- Editable firmware
- Custom samples
- Circuit board
- Customization
- Batteries
- Mini cable

Chico Bike Tunnel

12 06 22

He loved to run, at first it was because he was being chased, then because he was doing the chasing. It wasn't until his first year in Detroit that he saw a "90" stamped on his hand. He did have that little extra thing to play with but that was pretty small for a 20 year old. He trudged into the subway, sweaty and with his breath long and steady he perched himself near the tracks basking in the cool breeze, in sharp contrast to the world he just left. The payphone, behind him, slipped into his consciousness. There was someone talking in a half whisper.

"There's this tall man coming down the aisle, I think he may be my designated driver. I'm going down to the big city to have cocktails, there's a party where fellas drink martini sours, then wee on each other. If this tall man isn't my ride we might have to move it to February."

A Dramatic Interlude

12 03 22

I can't even remember who first suggested it,
but when he first walked out
in a dress to show a customer,
I saw what a good idea it was.
Anna Dodda Vida's Annual Fall Fashion Show
was about to get underway.
Cherry Cola had a problem on her hands.
One of her models was a no-show.
The model S0230 Serger is pre-lubricated at the factory.
Cherry obviously didn't like Meeks
who was the clear favorite.
Scuttlebutt has it that he thinks of himself
as a real ladies' man.
So, you never know, you might just get lucky tonight.
A lot of lint is produced
when the cutters are cutting the fabric.
As the bug strolled amid the meaty tissue
the mechanized tendrils positioned the fleshy arm
    back
into its position,
Naomi should be the standard for judging.
It was Saturday night.
Anna was in the mood for some rubbery fun.

She went to her large walk-in closet
and picked out the garments
for the evening's fun and games.
Somewhere over the Atlantic,
Maureen once again felt the need
to admonish her husband.
"Stop it! Stop playing with yourself
and get your hand out from under your skirt
before someone sees what you're doing!"
I decided to treat myself to this newer Serger.
It helped to watch a video regarding the lower looper.
Any thoughts on where we go
after this all settles down?
In the end, she decided on black rubber boots
with six-inch heels;
she sat on the edge of her bed
and pulled the shiny boots over her feet.
I'm behind on my sewing project,
a pretty little party dress,
and Governess is about to punish me
for not working faster.
Do I dread her firm hand on my bottom
or desire it?
It all culminated in a boring finale
where the wrong person won.

VHS Porn Stuck in the Machine

12 01 22

The Label puts out vaporwave music,
a loosely defined genre typified by echoey,
electronic ambient sounds and futuristic accompanying
   visuals.
It was a fun gig as a production assistant.
The show was basically bumpers edited around a
   crap movie.
Rhonda is fairly active on social media.
The idea of getting my hands on all these
obscure cassettes became this massive hobby.
I have an official promo tape from the Square Dancing
   Tractors.
I wonder if this was a craze.
I've been lucky enough to have seen *Zorn* a few times.
While this recording was stored on a special,
cutting-edge digital reel-to-reel tape recorder,
all input and output from the cameras & tape
was analog-component video
and the distribution formats were also all analog.

I recently was able to pick up a new laserdisc
which featured a very short segment
of Ronald Reagan's opening speech
for some convention in Las Vegas.
It's like a very pretentious demo of Video Toaster
or some similar editing system of the time.

A Fist Full of Oscillators

11 30 22

I recommend only letting people
at the age of seventeen see this.
It denotes the importance of good,
supportive, caring, and loving friends.
Singing a song called "Bubbles"
and making bubbling noises
during an oral sex scene
comes across pretty funny.
It teaches us to go after our goals,
to be diligent,
to never, ever give up.
On the Sabbath nearest to his thirteenth birthday,
the boy will become Bar Mitzvah
which means "Son of the Commandment."

Though it's clearly still
the best known adult movie of all time,
it cannot be called a good film
in any objective or traditional sense.

Eighty years ago, with no computer editing,
a simple narrative is crafted
with artisan ingenuity, effects, story telling, humor
and style with no equal.
This is toilet humor,
a dirty joke well told,
akin to the sauciness displayed
by burlesque comedians in between strip acts.
I'm sure that even those film buffs
personally unfamiliar with the film
are aware of what its title is alluding to,
but the uninitiated would not really be any the wiser
after having sat through it
in this truly lamentable guise.

A Slow walk to the Edge

11 15 22

The voltage that accompanies the CAT Rating isn't all that complicated. It's simply the maximum "working voltage" or "max line voltage" of the meter. Maximum surge and destructive voltage can be a little harder to find if not posted in the literature. He needs to be stuffed again. When I got there he had the hood up on his Semi and down on his pickup. The rig will just click when the key is turned. Sometimes you need a double helping of stuffing. We used PPS medium Auren in a fun way! I hooked it up and powered it on. It detected the battery and I got a "white light" indicating it was ready.

I suppose the difference in labeling is to say that it's not the same precision instrument that the "real" multimeters are. You can see the Cauca parallel to the Magdalena there but that's what isn't very clear in this map. What do the pink and blue mean? I like the reverse polarity protection mode that warns you if you connect it improperly. The Atacama desert is in northern Chile and it definitely doesn't reach the center. I purchased this booster and, after charging it completely, it started the car right up.

Vatican City Overture

09 27 22

I didn't realize how big it was until I bought it.
I took a Chance Unflared Extra Large,
proud to make it to the medial ring on the first go.
For most of human history
everyone smelled like a campfire.
An hour after a friend gave me his Sanwa Multimeter,
I wondered why I didn't get one sooner.
Now that we've finished our shower,
we just need to get it plumbed in.
I found that a rat or mouse was sneaking into the cab
at night.
I got a comment on one of my videos
from an account called Twitter Is Your Friend.
I finally got my replacement battery but it's acting
    funny.
Time to train,
I managed to take it all,
but still far from taking my horse dildo up to the base.
I'm so excited to share my latest beach video with you.
I have posted a few guides
for mods to the Marantz Cassette Deck,
for those of us who like to integrate tape
into our daily routine.

It looks like Twitter just added the Sanwa to the family.
Lying in bed enjoying the desert,
finally out of the cold that was making me miserable,
and here comes Mr. Dodge Ram.
Believe it or not the inspiration
to build out the attic space
came from an episode of the *Big Bang Theory*
where Penny was dressed in a leather domme outfit.
I've got my eye on the Gator Tri-Fold Tonneau
but I'd be interested in hearing
what others are looking at.
Before I started doing this,
I described getting rid of used sex toy
as "more difficult than disposing of nuclear waste"
because I lived on a military base
and security literally went through all the trash
before letting it leave.
I still need a lot of practice
for the really big things.

Duncanville, Texas

08 28 22

I opened my pants to gain relief before I sat. I'm not sure that you'd also get the clear "which one is the cinnamon roll" review readily available.

I think the height seems to be what strikes a chord for people, but hopefully this at least helps a bit. If you haven't tried it, you don't know what you're missing. Insanely good! I like it pretty well, but I wish there was a way to increase the volume of the Delay/Echo rather than use the Dry/Wet knob. "Some girl will be lucky to get you, Hudson." I said these words as tears filled my eyes.

It ranged from a serious discussion of why height differences may be emphasized in books to quips like "It's really not all that great being short because I cannot reach to throw things in the dumpster." The ideal size increases evenly and is pleasant in the sensations. I also have their Mic Mechanic, and I like it much better, but you can't switch from reverb to delay with a foot switch, so I use both boxes.

I watched as he peed, his now-soft cock curled in its four-inch length. I don't know if it's because I'm 5'9" or what, but it drives me up the wall reading about all these dainty little girls whose daintiness is what makes them cute and spunky. I keep the pedal at arm's height while standing so that I can adjust it on the fly, so I can't attest to how it stands up to multiple foot stomps. Do you need to go? I should be the spicy chick who works on cars and rides a motorbike. I don't play much live anymore.

Lubbock, Texas

Well he's a little fat but I wouldn't call him giant …
HOLY SHIT THATS A BIG DOG!
You look like you got your haircut
in an Icelandic prison.
Wipe that pout off your face, young lady!
From my seat I had a clear yet oblique view
of Man In A Dress and like a French fashion critic
I examined him in more detail.
I stood, then took off my uniform dress and blouse
revealing my slip, bra, and dainty petticoat.
They're also both absolutely gorgeous breeds,
and the Caucasians may
or may not have been specifically bred
for deterring wolves and bears.
You don't need the arrow
to remind guys your face is up there,
they're not looking at your tits.
I passed my work-seeker booklet through the slot
and our interview began.
You have to learn different stitches,
but it's not nearly as complicated
or scary as the machine.
It's just so much slower.

They're genetically predisposed to be independent
while watching flocks in the caucasus mountains
so they prefer to lead, not follow.
You look like you torture gingerbread men for
information.
Man In A Dress glanced over at me
and smiled the smile of an adolescent mountain beaver
remembering a night at a comedy club
and said, Tada!

Interesting Mall at Recife Antigo

08 16 22

To begin,
I am not a musician.

I took out a cute little floral cotton mini skirt,
one that just barely covered my ass
and didn't even manage that if a breeze blew.
I've spent hours
putting beats and chords together
sometimes not even really knowing what I'm doing.

I washed and touched every inch of her body
and watched as she changed.
She moved into my hands and yielded.
Seems like an easy request,
but unfortunately it took me several attempts
to find the right controller for my needs.

Next round I assume women's sizes and order a nine,
maybe nine and a half,
which should be a forty.
Maybe I can flash the cashier
and get you a discount on your ink cartridges.
Wrong, I get a forty two.

Carrot Cake with C.

Brian

08 14 22

Does Bird Person dream of Moclan cloaca?

olten, Switzerland

08 07 22

Maybe the Large seahorse I got will blow out my
    backside
enough to handle an Extra Large.
A famine due to a crop failure
might show as peak production.
I mainly got it for the noise. I'm gonna be loud.
Pads would miss trigger
when finger drumming
and the Polyphony is sixty-four.

After a few different synth tracks with chord,
melody and drum tracks
I would get drop outs.
We know the Aquifer is emptying at an alarming rate.
Sounds like fun either way.
You will need to scroll through a long list
or remember a saved project you created
in a custom synth in order to retrieve it.

Daingerfield, Texas

08 02 22

Foot is itchy and swollen after a night of camping. Found a plant this morning that I may have stepped in. I think my first glance of fetishism sparked when I watched "Flash Gordon" in something tight and shiny on television. One of the goals of the projected larger work is to make the case that reasonable religious believers ought to recognize that theistic arguments provide "no reason at all" for reasonable nonbelievers to change their minds.

They were originally named "The Vomit Pigs Make-Believe Blues Boobs Band." It's certainly sexy having plastic panties move around as you're in the heat of pleasing your partner—or yourself, on your own. There is a single concept of the infinite that is required to have application outside the philosophy of religion, and no concept that is inadequate to those external applications can be deemed adequate for the purposes of philosophy of religion. Someone taped themselves shooting a snake for no goddamn reason. PVC is my mayonnaise.

Hobart, Tasmania

He wished he could forget what had happened last night, or at least pretend that he hadn't seen his dad and Jack's Grandpa naked and doing only God knows what. Embrace your whimsical side wearing our Unicorn Dreams Onesie. Nothing is more subtle than a giant hole in the middle of a forest. Argghhh … shut up, I'll have nightmares!

Feel instantly happy and giddy as soon as you wear our Unicorn Twinkle—a vibrant vivid color teal. I liked the name of it too but until now didn't understand how justified of a name it was for a color like that. This is all just too much to think about. These bottoms have a high-waist cut, vinyl construction, semi-flare design, and hot pink fringe on the sides that sway to your every dance move. Many people assume they know the ocean, but they fail to respect the chaotic energy present and drown. Do you love him son?

Expand your experience and open up future opportunities within the Electronic Dance Music, Fashion, and Marketing industries. Not only will we love your bike, but there's a lot of good suggestions for tires on there. He'd come to grips with his dad's apparent sexuality and that he and Mack might be messing around, though he really didn't care to hear the details.

I have made so many lifelong friends around the country from being a Unicorn. I think what matters most to me is rolling resistance. Mack growled as he pushed into Mark's slick hole, his entire being concentrated on the seven inches he was slowly working into his partner. The hot pink crop top came with an attached hood with silver spikes, and the matching high-waist bottoms were accented with a tail and more dino spikes.

Bern, Switzerland – the Zytglogge

07 31 22

"It's me, Kane," his client confirmed,
clearing his throat.
"I'm in Switzerland."
In my country a lot of people
used to put fish in water wells,
mine included.
Now they all have populations of fish.
I wonder if some will survive
long enough to form new species.

The fetish club nearly closed
in two thousand nineteen
but managed to stay open
by charging for livestreams
of the pornographic partiers.
It was the most action I'd had
since Boris Johnson
announced the U.K. lockdown.

I am not selling my services,
I am just inviting you to visit the Clinic.

I feel like I'm making it up,
but it was real.
A former boyfriend told the court
that it seemed odd that my wife
would play the submissive role
as she was often a dominatrix
in their past encounters.
Any time our eyes met above the laptops,
I tried to diffuse the awkward silence
by blowing her a kiss or winking cheekily,
but her mouth just remained a grim straight line.
He learned more about being a woman
in that afternoon and evening
than in two weeks on the internet.
I've been playing too much *Horizon Forbidden West*.

At this point Hans Albert Einstein
was nearly completely nude,
wearing nothing but his soiled diaper,
a large weighted anal plug inside him,
and nipple clamps closed tightly
around his long moist nipples.
He went to his wardrobe
and fingered his way through Aunt Bea's clothes
just as she would.
The little fuzzball had on a red collar
which he tried to pry off using his back leg.
That's worth a shitload of money dude.

LMMS Bleary

07 19 22

Modern Romantic Satanism or Compassionate Satanism focuses on self-empowerment, science, and building social consciousness, while directly taking action. The Columbia Launch had fallen on hard times and the last day of the year was Valentine's Day.

The Silverbacks have arrived! Away with superstitions and fairy tales and in with solid ways to get involved in your own community for the good of all. Mostly, he wonders if there is some reason all the girls here have soft pale skin while their clients hold thick black cocks. It's the future. If you have never heard of Satanism, or social justice in general, this is perfect for you.

Got the tubes when I expected. I haven't posted for a while. Busy with HRT. Yeah, probably an ethical or existential problem somewhere in here, but apparently the ability for such self-reflection is a positive trait so no catatonic depression here. The only question I would have is why would the air nozzle thingy be so long, other than that they make a great low-cost replacement. Here lies a series of short essays about one person's journey of self-discovery through Ethical Satanism. Sissies in the Matriarchy just don't get a break. I look down at the scientist and ponder the believability of the situation. She certainly didn't look to be capable of building a laser gate.

Because human kindness ended up being her "higher power" in recovery, she is attempting to pay it forward by building community. She faces new challenges that force her deeper into her new role. This time, however, there seemed to be no immediate danger. I can't say fucking Adonis doesn't sound like a good time, but I've never been in a threesome.

All is good. I get about eight miles from home and down goes the front tire. We were the only freshmen invited. Was it possible that I was actually popular? Idly, she tried to guess what her summoner would want in exchange for his soul. He seems arrogant and self-absorbed, but who wouldn't be with a body like that? As you can see from the photos they're starting to bulge. You better get used to that, as pretty as you are it's bound to happen again. I can grant you power no king or emperor could ever possess. I can grant you riches beyond your imagination. Who cares if we're step brothers? We aren't actually related. I don't know why people gave negative reviews, as these are great and just as advertised.

Under the Help Desk

07 17 22

About three years ago
my mom bought me a Drive Transport Chair
for what we thought was just a lingering,
but short-term problem.
Most electronic music is too focused on vowels,
the tones and timbres.
They ignore the musical consonants—
how notes start, stop, and transition.
First-time home buyer here.
I've done the research,
and I'm ready to join the cult.
I bought a pillow to go in it.
My husband says it's very comfortable.
Now, let's imagine,
beyond the fallen walls,
dog owners paying attention to this message
while you are at your work
playing with machinery,
and they and them,
with open umbrellas,
taking pictures of our soul,
flesh and bones.

When I was in Boy Scouts,
I used to carry around a Swiss Army Knife.
I have a ton of issues.
I saw this when it was new,
and have re-watched *Performance*
more times than I can remember.
It's like an elderly car salesman
signing up a high-schooler to buy a lemon.
She has severe balance issues
and numbness in her feet and legs.
They don't make sounds like they used to.
Yep it's obvious in the movie
that Ursula is a bitch
and Ariel is an idiot.
I am not sure that I would recommend it for someone
who is wheelchair-bound
and needs to be in it all day and night.
The plot is loose,
but let's try to get somewhere.
Even more than wanting
to do the right thing for the environment,
I think this is a big and under-appreciated factor.
That means fewer tube failures,
fewer crashes,
and more safety built in
till the tire wears out.
I was looking and longing for
someone to do it right.

Like the old days.
I tossed a futon pad in my minivan for a few trips.
Dave said they were easy to handle
switching out roadside.
I don't know if it was your intention,
but as a forty-year-old man,
I cried during this amazing song.
I was always too tall
and they all looked girly
so I never had one,
but I remember them.

Save the Wails

07 13 22

She laughed
and it was like a thousand bells tinkling at once.
"This gin is very good."
I don't go to Taco Bell for quality eats,
I go for a cheap filling meal.
I like the size of the bells and they will work perfectly.
To make him appealing to other shemales and gays,
she gave him a drug
that would enhance his penis and testicles.

They are big, sturdy, and make a nice sound.
Karl will get married to that girl anyway.
They did the same with their radio stations too,
purged a few days after Bell Let's Talk Day.
It was exactly what I needed for a Christmas project.
Bells are going off in my head
as I hump my hips trying to ignore the bedspread
that's hanging over the foot of the bed.
I got more help from the cancellation department
since they actually got a real tech to figure out
that my modem wasn't functional.
There had been no red flags,
nothing to set alarm bells ringing.

I mean she routinely flies off
to war-torn countries to report on the news,
despite not really needing to at this point of her career.
A vampire battles the succubus
who killed his wife and son.
His car had all the latest bells and whistles,
including GPS.
I'm thinking about buying a small solar panel
for the top of the van, and then hooking it up to a
power converter
to continuously charge my batteries
throughout the day while I work.

What does it look like?
I am shaving my legs!

Jam Session

07 13 22

This machine is so '90s it's included TWICE in the
      name!
Can you imagine learning biology in high school
from a dude like this?!
What is this van called?
This unit really shines
when it's used with the intended signal path.
Kids are the most expensive things you can get for free.
This thing can't be that bad!
But wait! We have these pills now!
I'm so glad that Jerry and I
weren't left in suspense about the pizza.
It perfectly explained the mating habits
of a single-celled organism.
The Swiss must've been very confident in victory
if they included a corkscrew on their army knife.
There is a book titled *A Short History of Nearly Everything*.
It has a part where the author
talks to a guy who studies slime molds.
I bought a new edger,
it's the one that is multipurpose,
brand new out of the box.
"Tube-like snot condom" is a series of words
that will take the rest of my life to forget.

He's having some fun with my dildo, who's next?
I had no bloody clue what it meant in the nineties,
and watching this made me realize
I'm still totally baffled.
I did my senior project on *Dictyostelium discoideum*
when I was a biology major at the Air Force Academy.
That sounded like something Picard would say.
My Integra and considerably older Triton rack
are still in frequent use.
Perhaps the Triton would make a good episode.
When I was in college, I had a professor
who genuinely used *True Facts* in his lesson plans.
Dad, look at that car!
It looks like an angry beaver!
I hope some day some of these old ROMpler engines
and tone banks
get re-released in some way,
either as a plugin or some kind of throwback gadget.
Runaway dog penis!

Touching

07 12 22

Seeing the oven on the first pic was slightly unsettling.
Sleeping is actually kinda scary,
you have no guarantee you're going to wake up,
you're completely vulnerable
and a lot of things can happen.
I usually post weekly,
I bought a new hot Victoria's Secret outfit for a set.
I'd rather just get sushi for dinner and not do it.
My motivation is gone.
The manual says it takes 14 feet of line,
and EGO sells replacement line pre-cut to 14 feet,
but I saw a YouTube video
that said that it could take up to 30 feet.
Honey is the tastiest insect vomit in the entire world.
Want to see a naughty little school girl?
I would have thought these sort of rules
would already be in place
and were just not enforced.
How tall are Pokémon by generation?
A year ago the local television station
was giving these buttons and stickers out
at a Comic-Con I attended.

Here's a Lo-Fi Sample Pack
filled with some instrumental loops I recorded.
Someone misnamed Country Hills as "Crunchy Hills."
What other creative modifications can you think of
for Calgary neighborhoodUs?
Do Tape Machines Dream of Electric Bleeps?
Can I make you hard?
I picked up my Maverick if anyone cares.
She saved the *Orville* and crew from death
and created a new timeline where they are all alive.
None of your boot-licking ignorance
is even remotely conclusive.
Every day I wake up
with this massive clitoris throbbing
between my legs, and the realization
that I'm exposing more and more of myself.
My wife and I had just visited our Lowe's
to see the new Oldsmobiles in person.
We took pictures and measurements
to make sure it would fit in our garage.
Finished my first lot of spanking paddles,
I like how they turned out.
The light shows green when I check it
but when I use it,
it dies almost instantly.
I recently had my best week on the porn site,
where I made more money than I ever have,
and now this week I'm super low.

Twenty thirty has become such a poster child
for future predictions
the actual year itself is going to pale
in comparison to all the hype around it.
In fact, I am appalled at the idea
of even thinking like that.

Jack's Grandpa Has Very Soft Skin

07 10 22

Bathhouse clientele are more likely to engage in casual sex with random people. All that was about to change. One day I purchased a local Adult Oriented Newspaper that catered to fetishes and other adult pleasures. Oil is relatively cheap but oil changes are expensive, and my local quick oil change franchise sometimes didn't put the care into my car that I would prefer. I know it's been a few years, and that you'd changed your name, but I'm really curious about it all. In fact, I'd like a close examination. I didn't answer the ad for a couple weeks because the idea of being dressed up by someone the age of my grandfather seemed odd. There are specific venues called gay saunas/bathhouses that are designed for sex.

As soon as I got into my apartment I dialed his number. The moment the telephone rang I lost my nerve and hung up. A pert set of small breasts with big nipples and a shrinking waistline outweighs my small penis. For engine or transmission oil extraction, your car needs a dipstick. Cialis sounds better to me. A little safer, but you have to know how to use it, too.

I don't see the huge sacrifice myself, she earns more here than in the States because the competition isn't as fierce. Me being me for my first oil change using it, I drained it with the extractor until it was completely drained. Sex is only natural, I'm not doing anything embarrassing on those videos. Stacks of 30 sheets are very securely held together with a "MICRO" size BINDER CLIP. I wouldn't be surprised if he uploaded it somewhere.

He gave me a quick tour of the house and led me upstairs to the washroom. I was told to shower and then come down to the first door on the right. It struggled on my wife's car, the tube would not reach the bottom of the sump but I've used a crap one of these before so I have a silicon tube that I attached to the tube that came with the "sucker." It settles in the hot oil in the bottom of the pan, job done. I would have liked the sizes to be distributed a little more evenly, but I knew the quantity of each size I was getting by reading the description.

Rings and Things

07 06 22

I still remember the first time one of the boys in my class asked me to touch his penis, he was just a year older than me. I think it gives it a slight tug cause of how the balls tend to retract into your body when you cum so those stop that. Give it a try, see if it's your thing. It's a little challenging to measure silicone with calipers, but these seem to be pretty much exactly as specified. The next few moments are a bit hazy to me as I just stood there with cum dripping down my face. Even if you are very careful not to screw the cap onto the bottle tightly, you will get rubber dust in your drink. Now I had nursed at a woman's breast, masturbated her and came in Scooter's mouth for our first ever oral. I have no clue how to get the right size. The silicone one keeps pulling on my hair and the metal one is too big.

I am on birth control. You desperately shove your dick into a wad of toilet paper, but that only makes your balls hurt. My mom bought these for the transmission cooling lines on her Audi A4, they looked slightly bigger than the original, but after installing, it held up nicely with no leaks. "Let's get started." Sally said. We have all night. Eventually, you stop thinking. The rubber rings on the legs of my 12-year old Joby GorillaPod had deteriorated and become sticky. I turned to see Scooter's brother and John, his best friend, staring open-mouthed at the three of us. "Don't go putting this on me, like I've somehow gone out of my way to surprise you. I've got places to be, man."

The two-inch auger is perfect for this task. It goes into the soil like a hot knife through butter. I wondered why they were here. I can't be playing hide-the-actual-salami with the Terminator's younger, shittier cousin. I would recommend saving the plastic foil that covers the suction cup. I felt his hard penis against mine. I knew this was where I belonged. This and the Don Quixote show that Penis Garrison has zero reading comprehension skills. Of course you can swap the battery to keep recording. Come up next to me. One of you on each side. Suck later.

This has been a quick reminder that if you have to label the political messages in your drawing, they may not be as effective as you think.

Where Good Men Die

06 19 22

I had two projects in mind when choosing this collection.
I have no idea if the people writing about Jeeps
are trying to be funny,
but they should probably get some sleep.
He sounded like a total airhead.
What had that thing done to him?
The inside isn't finished/coated
to prevent rusting like the outside.
Use your voice to make things dramatic
or funny or whatever
so that the young listener/reader
can really enjoy the story along with you.
I tried not to look too much
at the fucked up milieu
of perversion around me as I ran.
How was that supposed to make it better?
The two men remained
seated in the tub for several minutes
relaxing and absorbing the warm caress of the mud.
I lay on my bed with the room spinning
and pulled up Grindr.
My wife is just in love with this trash can.
Yes, she actually said that.

Apparently I was really into chest hair.
Who knew?
"Sheep in a Jeep was one of her favorites long ago."
Why did I say that?
This was weird as fuck.
It was like the touch of her memory
had warped all of history.
Will purchase again.
No scratches.
No dents.
None of that!
Period!

None of Them Knew

06 19 22

There are many people who are probably jealous
that you can speak your native language
with such ease.
Well at least Lowe's decided to bring that
janky assed whatever you call it down.
There's an ALT button on the back
that doubles up the presets
recalled through the toggle switch.
I'll bet humans had on average,
longer fingernails prior to clippers being invented.
Score of your fantasy football matchup?
Tomorrow is my birthday
and I want to be a live stream.
What should I do live?
Second month in Calgary, and Dave is not taking it well.
Ship is finished,
but what is your worst encounter?
A lot of ancient languages
were probably the way they are
because people had no teeth.
Birthdays are actually a date not a day.
Yeeeh!

Drink your meals.
Within a few years
CAPTCHAs will be completely useless.
It's the 7-year anniversary
of this large funnel cloud over the city.
Would love to see a video
digging deeper into the software.
Could I use hair dye
instead of normal dye for dying a shirt?
Folks tend to focus too much on weirdness
during synth pedal demos.
It is exceedingly likely
there are female Kaylon models somewhere.
Porn is the most researched subject ever.
What do you all think?

Spanking the Thingy

05 31 22

I chose the color royal blue, in size medium,
according to my measurements in the table
I am entirely medium.
If you like more fitted,
a size small would be perfect.
These discs do wear but last a long time
compared with other options.

As he prepares to start work as an aerobics instructor
Klyton wistfully ponders his training days in the
    lavatorial sciences.
Our clothing may run larger or smaller than the size
    you normally wear.
They should get rid of the fishing tackle style box,
which is really too large for what it contains.
It includes the themes of cuckolding, drugs, blackmail,
    and sissification.
This will lead to exploitation and organized crime in
    future episodes,
an indication of the mixture of drugs and hormones
    used
will become more apparent by then.
Buy the premium and don't try saving your money.
There is no Silicone Heaven.

Cacophony of Zoom

05 30 22

Four knobs control all the parameters of your sound
    creation.
I made sure to have her request it
just so we could delight in my Jeff
rolling on the floor in anguish
at the prospect of having to read "Scuffy" once again.
As he tenderly squeezed Julia's breast
he started thumbing her spongy nipple,
I grabbed one of the medium sized boxes
and climbed on the ladder to slide it onto the loft.

Four knobs control all the parameters of your sound
    creation.
"Glad to meet you Brian," Julia said as she began to
    strip off her clothes.
This is good for someone who wants to explore
    modulation
before spending a bunch of money.
I may have not followed the instructions
on how to apply it appropriately,
although I don't think there were instructions for that.
Scuffy turned and saw Vinton,
he remembered Vinton but only vaguely.
I ordered the first unit and it was dead on arrival.

omnichord Sextape

05 01 22

Marvin had always been a transvestite,
but today he was taking this identity,
this proclivity, to work.
Everything about his mundane job seemed new.
Screens, lights, and knobs reflected through sticky
    eyelashes
carried an exciting energy
as if they hadn't been there the day before,
and the day before that.

"I enjoy the music that you play.
I'm always impressed by the sounds you get.
This one in particular has a feature set
that I couldn't imagine,
but you make it sound killer."
He lost track of what Elizabeth was saying.
What was her motivation?
What did she want out of this?
Marvin couldn't imagine someone like Liz
speaking to him without some level of sarcasm.

Oblivious to the storm of feelings brewing behind
    his eyes,
Elizabeth continued,
"I really like the use of momentary tremolo
on the distorted bass line.
It added some good life to the ambient destructive bed
for the melody above it."

Marvin's mouth opened and began to speak
as if reciting some passage from some forgotten book.
"It's experimental sound collage of acoustic folk songs
with some digital manipulation,
blessed by cassette tape.
It was an expression of my feelings at the time.
but hopefully you can get something out of it too."

Sexy Times in the Laundry Room

04 29 22

I've reached some wacky plateau
with the number of voice tracks totally wrecked in
    one bit of music.
It took me a while to see the drone/baseline sound
as a feature not a bug.

Not easy.
The medium itself can come over as an artificial
    afterthought.
Aiming for something you see in your head, but
    ending up somewhere else.

Once you eroticize the constant droll,
and the horrible lighting,
maybe nothing else will do.
Somebody called it an exposed insulation,
a mariachi adventure,
but of course I paid them to say that.

A Twist of Wire

04 19 22

Silicone is ALWAYS preferable for cleanliness, zero odor, and super-tough durability. A spring by any other name, handlebars need be installed. So when dual layer silicones hit the market I was glad to see it. I like bottoming out on the balls and that's no fun if you're past your comfortable depth. I did have a few issues during installation. If the WD-40 does not work, use a penetrating oil at the top and bottom to loosen the track.

Sheepherder

04 19 22

There's so much that can happen.
Throw some delay, reverb, et cetera in line.
You'll be bordering on that scene from *Deep Throat*
when the dude's eyes roll back in his head.

The overall volume of the synth can be controlled
using the built in VCA with an external control
   voltage.
When the VCA is inactive MIVEC outputs sound
   continuously.

As most of our healing Crystals are natural,
they are each unique.
Hence why no two Crystal pendants will be alike.
They may have minor chips or scratches
every penis has its own natural colors and patterns.

Part 1 – Talks with Gloria

03 13 22

Had I known what to look for with spade bits,
hole saws, and self-feed bits,
I might have spent the afternoon fishing
instead of cussing and swearing.

The largest spade bits typically require low-speed
    mode
to deliver the required torque to the bit.
Collectively, we usually refer to the whole thing as
    a hole.
What do you mean you don't do that?
Seriously, you're kidding right?

Part 2 - Talks with Gloria

03 15 22

I assumed "long term use"
referred to one's ass and not to prep,
so I was very confused
as to how it could result in kidney/liver damage.
They offered to compensate me for my problem.
If I accept that offer, most likely, they will want me
    to update my reviews and rating.

So far none of them have pinned
meaning no teeth have stripped off.
Great value compared to the lot-lizards.
The guy is just being honest.
Very Christian of him, in fact.
Maybe my mind is in the gutter.
The photo doesn't match what I received.

I guess it's my fault
for buying a blow up doll to begin with.

Part 3 - Talks with Gloria

03 15 22

If I accept that offer, most likely, they will want me to update my reviews and rating. I guess it's my fault for buying a blow up doll to begin with. Peering through the moss you discover, of all things, a pearl to be kissed. At first, lighting wasn't nearly as complicated as it is today.

Part 4 – Talks with Gloria

03 15 22

Peering through the moss you discover,
of all things,
a pearl to be kissed.
Seriously, you're kidding right?

At first, lighting wasn't nearly as complicated as it
    is today.
The largest spade bits
typically require low-speed mode
to deliver the required torque to the bit.
Collectively, we usually
refer to the whole thing as a hole.

What do you mean
you don't do that?

Trapped with Karen

03 07 22

Into this simple storyline,
he packs an astonishing mix
of sadness, yearning, humor, and kick-ass songs
with a little Platonic philosophy
tucked inside for good measure.

Wind pushes into me,
I am a sail for the wrong direction.

What do you think?
Do you think love lasts forever?

Legs spinning madly
the constant fluid movement
I'm pedaling nonstop.

A Walk into Bikini Beach

03 06 22

I know, it's weird, and maybe I wouldn't actually
  enjoy it?
You can see it's activated
when you see some somewhat translucent purple
  shield fragments
things floating around an enemy.
Sandy accepts she is a woman now
and gets ready to greet Marie's friend
dressed as a German barmaid.
I saw one at the Denver show a few years back
going for $2,000.
I wanted to inject humanity into an artificial system.
It was only a little bigger than the piece shown here.
I guess I can't know unless I put the ideas out there
and see who bites.
Make it like Metal Gear, so you can Velma
but you've got a fuckin' piece on you,
and just blast the ghosts
while you try to find those damn glasses.

All we can do is get to know and love the person
    looking back at us,
but just remember that while you're constantly
    growing older,
it's a chance to do and become something new in
    the process.
I would love to show this to my geology professor
but the name reminds me why I won't.
FUCK IT. No one else cares.

I was blown away at how the world was so clear.
Being able to read text on a screen is awesome as well.
This whole arc will take three volumes.
You have been warned.
Take the time to remember everything that you've done
and be ready for the next part of your journey.
The villain steals her glasses,
and the entire game is a violent quest to get them back,
because they're expensive.

Vallejo Trip Redux

02 11 22

A long strange trip to Vallejo,
Jamie still gets annoyed at being stuck
in the artificial traffic they intentionally created.
It is still a little awkward to talk about the details of
    my body.
When Craig and his friend Lucy land in a car accident,
Craig awakens from a coma.
Hilarious.

Use with a Violet Wand and Body Contact Cable,
and Indirect or Reverse Techniques
to electrify your own touch and make the sparks,
or you can scratch with our Queen Nails without
    electrifying them.

You're at a party, maybe drinking a little more than
    you should
one of your friends says let's go on a booze run
and grab some more drinks,
you hop in the car.
Use with Reverse Technique for freedom of movement,
but it can also be used indirectly.
Broadly speaking, the aim of hybrid cars
is to reduce tailpipe emissions
and reduce traditional fuel consumption,
allowing the potential for reducing motoring costs

and the ability to reduce air pollution in some
    situations.
This is just a way for them to easily charge you with
    something
so they can hold you whilst they gather more evidence.
I'm only in 14th place!
This means you can drive away from home
knowing you have a full battery.

I usually prefer a naturally born woman,
to a Venusian simulation.
Although I will admit I did make it with Jeff
when he was Lucy that one time.

You didn't commit a terrorist act yet,
and depending on the circumstances
you may not have gotten close enough to success
to be guilty of attempted terrorism.
You had bad thoughts,
but without a provable bad act,
you haven't committed a crime.
I will not describe how I shower.
It is still a little awkward to talk about the details of
    my body.
After a short spell of driving,
the battery can transfer power to the electric motor,
helping the car move along in traffic, when parking,
or if you hit the accelerator to gain speed,
giving the engine a boost and saving fuel.
You think I haven't heard the rumors yet?

Admit it, you just want me as a
bed-bunny for your harem.
We should all start going onto them interwebs
and relentlessly plugging.
I would like for us to become closer in the future,
but only when you are ready.
I can wait.
Just give me a sign when you are ready.
I decided that I'd like to have more tools
and develop the skills to use them,
but now was not the time.

Lovers from a Past Life

01 30 22

Greg thinks he wants shoelaces, but he can't find the cobbler shop in the mall. Fortunately for Greg, he finds a different store.

The Wizard won't sell him any laces, but the Wizard also knows what Greg really wants. There was a sickness though the country hate was prevalent and war was imminent. Greg had some of this madness, his mother was warned. She would get the memories of Aaron, whom she used to be. Things get crazy in a hurry, with Kasumi going as far as acting as though she was still him. She is even given a chance to be Gregg again. Swapping bodies with Barbara seemed like a good idea at the time.

She came in through the Bathroom Window (Ruined Cover)

01 30 22

I have a very cute friend who literally crawled through a bathroom window recently. Since hearing about it, this song has been a constant earworm. I decided I should record it myself in hopes that it'll go away.

The orgy of the ood

01 26 22

Setting the ignition contact point gap may eventually
    become a lost art,
since the points are replaced in modern cars by
    electronic ignition.
Some owners of classic cars find it more practical
to replace the points with an aftermarket system.

I drank my morning smoothie with a profound sense
    of dread.
I knew the change was coming but we pretended we
    didn't know.
Maybe hope and delusion go hand in hand.
Up until a week ago, I believed the new owners of
    my company,
Deutschland Distributors, were a chain of retail
    outlets based in Germany.
That was not the case.

The best way is to remove them from the distributor
if it's possible to do this without damage.
If the dwell angle is not the same for all cylinders,
the result is rough running and poor fuel economy
because the moment the spark-plug fires
varies from cylinder to cylinder.

The fluid amount used in this type of takeover
is five hundred to one thousand milliliters.
The doctors may ask you to hold the fluid in your
    anal opening
for a long time to release the stool completely.
It stimulates the lining of the colon to cause bowel
    movements.

Heroic Product Demo Music

01 11 22

Loathe sex is strange sex.
Everyone should experience it at least once.
Not really fun, but what you learn about yourself after.

My XL should be built soon.
Fully loaded, minus about 5 or 6 cables.

Her parents are forcing her to get married at the
young age of 22.
I tried giving her advice on what to do but she plainly
rejected my every idea and started ignoring me.

Like being crazy, horny is the hyper-sexual end of
the pool and post-nut clarity is the shallow end.
The real base position should be just not especially
turned on or satisfied.
17th-century Dutch scientist Antonie van Leeuwenhoek
had the post-nut clarity to collect some of his own
nut juice and put it under a microscope.
The existence of pre-nut confusion and post-nut clarity
implies that there is such a thing as mid-nut learning.

I'm a pastor and put a lot of miles on my vehicle.
Gets even better mileage towing a trailer than my
Hyundai Santa Fe.

Yeah, in this context OC means that what you are
    posting is yours.
In terms of art it can also mean that your work is not
    inspired by any existing piece.
Clearly you did nothing wrong, but you have some
    very valid feelings.

I've been making stronger boundaries with subs lately.
It's so hard.

I would love to spend a couple hours poking around
    that thing.
Look at that antenna on the nose.

An Addict Dreams of Pantyhose

01 09 22

The wide elastic straps will accommodate most sizes, and the attractive thong style back design offers snug maneuverability.

Insert a flared-base dildo into one of the included metal O-rings, snap it into place, and you are ready.

I have many photos of cars and emblem detail shots that are not on Etsy.

After a good ass flogging, Exxon enthusiastically returns the favor by servicing Minnie with some pussy licking before Marvin takes it over with face-sitting and a hot sixty-nine.

The other stroker is open-ended to pleasure the entire shaft, lined with stimulating nubs for a massage with every thrust.

Enjoy an intense vibrating experience, solo or shared!

2021

The Bells the Bells

12 26 21

Due to his high karma, he has "near-limitless possibilities for reincarnation." He chooses to reincarnate in a fantasy world as a voluptuous futanari-succubus with big tits and an irresistible smile.

A shameless, desperate, bitter, angry creep gets exactly what he deserves after he tries to take it by force.

She's wearing a plain, white t-shirt that only comes down to mid-hip and a pair of teal panties. At least I think they're teal. Could be turquoise? Like I said before, I'm not great with colors.

I guess I was so preoccupied with getting to my destination, I forgot to fill it up. My car came sputtering to a halt right at the entrance to a forest trail. I ended up not having any reception out there and wondered what I was going to do.

Sighing heavily, I put my hands on my hips.

Ecclesiastical Nipple Clamps

12 26 21

Every now and then I get a real need for bells.
How do you get more medium than medium?
Took it home and placed it in a jar
with a rubber seal and metal clamp.
The bottle is new with the plastic seal.
When I opened her today I could smell the liquid.
100mg per day was the cure.
Been around for a while.
Much of its magic
is its ability to increase O_2 levels.
The brain is the only organ
that knows about its own existence.
My latest find is "Foggy Notion" by The Velvet
Underground.
My ears pricked up on hearing it on the radio
just the other day.
Her rope skills are amazing
and she has tried most everything kink-wise.
She is tall, brunette and has big beautiful brown eyes.
She has amazing legs and an even better butt.

Funky Tape Lofi

12 25 21

She-Ra has a rigorous interview process for this little slut to find out if she is worthy of her time and dungeon.

The two share a rather comical but nonetheless touching moment together before arriving at the chapel.

Down the aisle, along with Sophia, the girls think to themselves about the beautiful friendship they shared.

Bertha boasts she's really good at making lattes but by the end of the day she'll be good at getting her crème whipped.

The girls seemed to be really into each other.

Miss Maizel was doing some awesome things with her mouth.

Whether portrayed by people or puppets, the show's four main characters are always presented as roommates, best friends, even chosen family members, all of them effectively single.

A Nightmare in Mauve

12 21 21

Some people could argue that real dreams have deeper meanings, but in a story, they really have to have a clear purpose. You're having the worst nightmare ever. And finally you manage to wake up. You are sweating profusely. You wonder whether it was a dream or an actual incident. My main character is having a nightmare about the beginning of World War 3. We know forces are at work that hold them in a tight grip.

When Hubble sends back a snapshot of stars in an ocean of darkness, the improbability is what makes a mark. Bob Vila glanced out the star-speckled window, drinking in the sight of the drops splattering in the sky.

A nightmare or dream is like any other scene in a book or story. There should be a point or purpose.

Wavehub Gain TIDDI

12 07 21

A li'l less chaotic than some of my recent fare. I was imagining a long intro to some giant crash, but then I couldn't bring myself to break this moment.

Bloopus Bebop

12 06 21

Inspired by a new site I found, which will doubtless trigger a longer story, or more than one, in the weeks to come. I find the whole concept of faith driving the change of gender to be quasi-Canadian.

Unfortunately, many of us do not put the time into proper maintenance, and our hands and feet start to look old before their time. If you don't take care of your hands and feet, they'll turn dry and flaky. Neglecting them will also lead to skin cracking around the nails, which can be painful. Fortunately, there are many things you can do every day to better care for your hands and feet.

There are two places you'll need to measure, waist and hips. Your waist measurement will be taken across the narrowest part of your lower torso, likely an inch or two below your belly button. Your hip measurement will be taken in the same way, but around the widest part of your lower torso, similar to where you wear your jeans. Make a note of the measurements in both inches and centimeters; depending on the brand, either could be useful.

Pitfalls of Dialup

12 03 21

Noise Music is a genre of music that is characterized by the use of noise within a musical context. This type of music tends to challenge the distinction that is made in conventional musical practice between musical and non-musical sound, with unforeseen consequences.

A brilliant general forced to flee during the clone war and assume an identity he never expected, will receive a break from her maschalagnia to realize some of the women involved might have been blonde.

Life is not a bed of roses for a bathmophobic construction worker, not even a good one.

The newly hired diplomat is put to work with his first client. But could it be this easy? He receives an email as Kelly and Miley take over the lives of a lot of people in the world struggling with Morton's neuroma.